persuasive
genre
informational
poetry
fiction

First
Next
Then

What the
**Science
of Reading**
Says
about

Writing

Jennifer Jump, M.A., and Hillary Wolfe, M.A.

Other Books in This Series

Contributing Author

Kim Carlton, M.Ed.
Richardson, Texas

Contributors

Amy Piecuch
Former Middle School Teacher
Fox River Grove Middle School, Illinois

Amy Sroka
Former Fourth Grade Teacher
The Leffell School, White Plains, New York

Publishing Credits

Corinne Burton, M.A.Ed., *Publisher*
Aubrie Nielsen, M.S.Ed., *EVP of Content Development*
Emily R. Smith, M.A.Ed., *SVP of Content Development*
Véronique Bos, *VP of Creative*
Cathy Hernandez, *Senior Content Manager*
Jill Malcolm, *Graphic Designer*
David Slayton, *Assistant Editor*

Image Credits: pp. 33, 54, 60, 65, 86, 96, 103 Jennifer Jump; all other images Shutterstock and/or iStock

Shell Education

A division of Teacher Created Materials
5482 Argosy Avenue
Huntington Beach, CA 92649-1039
www.tcmpub.com/shell-education
ISBN 978-1-0876-9671-3
© 2023 Shell Educational Publishing, Inc.
Printed in USA. WOR004

Table of Contents

Table of Contents *(cont.)*

Introduction

Welcome from Jen Jump

The Hippocratic oath is powerful. Most of us have heard it spoken of, usually in passing, perhaps while watching a medical drama on television. We often think of the oath in terms of the simple phrase "Do no harm." The reality is that the oath is much more substantive. The language is intense, lofty, and powerful. According to tradition, medical professionals have been swearing some form of the Hippocratic oath since the fourth century BCE. Without parsing out the implications and utility of the oath to modern-day medicine, most people know its purpose and relevance.

The current version of the oath (revised in 1964) articulates several thoughtful tenets that stand out:

1. **I will respect the hard-won scientific gains of those physicians in whose steps I walk, and gladly share such knowledge as is mine with those who are to follow.**

   Yes! I want every doctor I meet to listen to the knowledge gained from the physicians who went before them. I want my medical professionals to share what they learn from diagnosing and treating me. In the same way, I want that for my educator friends. I want us all to remember that the successes and failures of the educators who have gone before us, the hard research studies undertaken, and the seminal understandings gained pave the way for us. Many scholars have shown us the way over the years, with the goal of ensuring that we use these bodies of knowledge and understanding to provide the best for our students.

2. **I will remember that there is art to medicine as well as science, and that warmth, sympathy, and understanding may outweigh the surgeon's knife or the chemist's drug.**

While medicine is largely clinical (the science), there is an art to it that includes listening, considering, and understanding. Realizing there is an art to teaching creates the possibility of joy and passion, along with challenge and precision. It is the art, when matched with the science in education, that ensures that students are considered first. It ensures that families and caregivers are seen as partners and that the classroom is a dynamic place for all.

3. **I will not be ashamed to say, "I know not," nor will I fail to call in my colleagues when the skills of another are needed for a patient's recovery.**

It is my hope that a doctor, when stymied by a condition or illness, will be open to the support of a colleague, optimally one who has researched the condition or has a deeper understanding based on experience. Educators, too, should strive for the candor of asking for help and for the willingness to listen. As professionals, each time we open a professional resource, read a research article, or engage in professional learning, we are acknowledging that there is more to know.

In essence, the oath speaks to us, as educators. We can align our professionalism to that of medical professionals. We, too, consistently promise to "do no harm." We create classrooms filled with joy and learning, love and laughter, and rigor and challenge. While there is no formal oath for teachers, each day upon beginning class, we promise to listen to the wisdom of the research, to remember the art and science of the work we do, and to be unafraid of requesting help when needed. We are dedicated.

It is not always easy. Sometimes, the research is complex, confusing, or seems contradictory. Education can be a whirlwind. Standards change. Curriculum changes. Expectations change. Legislation changes. And lately, these changes are compounded by added pressures. But the need for young people to develop literacy skills does not waiver. Reading, writing, speaking, and listening consistently reign as must-have skills.

Several years ago, I stood on a stage in front of eager educators, ready to begin the new year. We were talking about literacy, engaged in the conversation around the importance of reading challenging texts. Education was in the midst of change, and for many, it was an intense, scary change. The research (what we now call "the science") was indicating the need for systemic change. We needed then, as educators need now, to be ready, willing, and able to heed the research and orchestrate instructional change within our classrooms. The purpose of this book is to support that goal.

What Is the Science of Reading?

This book is one in a series of professional resources that provides a close look at the discussion around the Science of Reading (SOR). What exactly does that mean? The term the *Science of Reading* pervades the national conversation around the best literacy instruction for all students. The purpose of this series is to close the gap between the knowledge and understanding of what students need to become

> We create classrooms filled with joy and learning, love and laughter, and rigor and challenge.

literate humans and the instructional practices in our schools. This gap is widely acknowledged yet remains largely intact. While research is available, journals are not easy to navigate. "It would be the proverbial needle in a haystack problem trying to find the most relevant information" (Kilpatrick 2015, 6). With concise resources that build understanding of the body of research, however, teachers can be equipped with the logical steps to find success. Mark Seidenberg notes, "A look at the basic science suggests specific ways to promote reading success" (2017, 9).

The great news is that this book will help you navigate the important research that informs the Science of Reading conversations. Let's begin by quickly breaking down the words behind the hype: the *Science of Reading*.

> **Science:** a branch of knowledge or study dealing with a body of facts or truths systematically arranged and showing the operation of general laws or systematic knowledge of the physical or material world gained through observation and experimentation
>
> **Read[ing]:** looking at carefully so as to understand the meaning of (something written, printed, etc.) (Dictionary.com 2022)

Bottom line? The Science of Reading is the collection of excellent research that leads to the understanding of how students learn to read. What are the best ways to support students as they break down the code of the English language? How can teachers provide the best instruction for developing fluency? What are the structures within text and embedded within instruction that will best support students as they decipher text and develop the skills to understand a range of genres in various contexts and content areas? Which strategies will best help students develop the ability to write with adequate voice, grammatical control, and knowledge? The answers are found in the collection of research, studies, and experiences (the ultimate educators of the universe) known as the Science of Reading. Many of the research studies have been duplicated, reinforcing the understanding of how students learn to read.

To be clear, nothing about this body of work is brand new. There are ebbs and flows within any conversation, and while some of the conversations around the SOR have resurfaced in recent times with great enthusiasm and debate, the basic components of this body of research have been discussed among literacy researchers and educators for many years.

Figure I.1—Components of Literacy

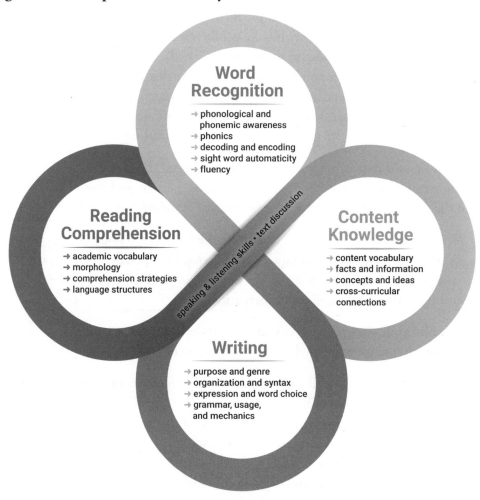

Figure I.1 demonstrates an approach to linking the research-based components of the Science of Reading, highlighting word recognition, reading comprehension, content knowledge, and writing. A very intentional decision has been made to include the science of *literacies*, including reading and writing as well as recognizing the power of speaking and listening, in this series. Each book will explore instructional implications, best practices, and things to look for in classrooms, as well as identify educational practices to reconsider. (To best incorporate pedagogical practices, reading comprehension and content knowledge are presented in one book.) These books were developed to support professional growth, enhance engagement, and provide support in designing instruction that incorporates the best researched-based strategies.

This research base and understanding are integral to instruction in today's classrooms. Yet, despite a general knowledge of these ideas, many students continue to be plagued by inadequate literacy skills. Pulling from the work of educators, psychologists, neurologists, special educators, and more, our hope is that a renewed focus on the science ("body of facts or truths") of literacy will support a change in instructional practices and lead to higher literacy achievement.

> " Being an expert reader doesn't make you an expert about reading. That is why there is a science of reading: to understand this complex skill at levels that intuition cannot easily penetrate. "
> —Mark Seidenberg (2017, 4)

Seminal Works to Build Understanding

Foundational works set the tone for understanding how research illuminates the pathway for instruction within the classroom. These seminal, theoretical pieces of research are widely recognized and serve as the guides to the books in this series. We will begin the journey with research and theories from the mid-1980s. Philip Gough and William Tunmer's seminal model of how young people learn to read, the Simple View of Reading (SVR), builds our understanding in a simple and usable manner (1986). This widely used model has been manipulated to support new models since its origination. The Simple View of Reading articulates the basic components of how people become comprehenders of text.

Figure I.2—Simple View of Reading

Decoding	×	Language Comprehension	=	Reading Comprehension

Research indicating that reading comprehension is the product of decoding (word-level reading) and language comprehension is showcased in an equation that defines the skills needed to become a reader (Gough and Tunmer 1986). The idea presented by the SVR is that strong reading comprehension depends on both decoding and language comprehension being present and strong. When one component is absent, reading comprehension will not occur. Although they are depicted simply in figure I.2, the skill domains of decoding and language comprehension include complex constructs that need to be understood separately and in relation to other constructs. *Decoding* (word level reading) includes print concepts, phonological awareness, phonics and word recognition, and word knowledge. *Language comprehension* includes background knowledge, academic language, academic vocabulary, inferential language skills, and narrative language skills. Intentionally represented as multiplicative rather than additive, the Simple View of Reading highlights that reading comprehension is a result of both successful decoding and comprehension.

In 2001, Hollis Scarborough expanded on the foundation of the SVR in an effort to better support parents in understanding how children acquire the skills to be successful readers. Her Reading Rope shows how the skills of word recognition and language comprehension come together to support proficient reading. Not only are the many components of decoding and language comprehension interrelated, the two skill areas must be integrated for reading comprehension to take place.

The lower strands of the rope represent *word recognition*, weaving together phonological awareness (awareness of sounds within words), decoding (an understanding that sounds are encoded and decoded by the alphabet), and sight recognition (automaticity with frequently used words). These strands braid together as the portion of the rope that ensures students can pull print from texts.

The upper strands of the rope signify *language comprehension*. These include background and content knowledge, vocabulary, language structures, verbal reasoning, and literacy knowledge. These strands articulate the range of comprehension skills, strategies, and knowledge that support reading with fluency and understanding.

Figure I.3—Scarborough's Reading Rope

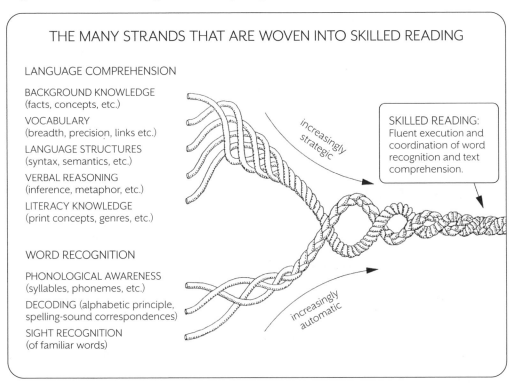

THE MANY STRANDS THAT ARE WOVEN INTO SKILLED READING

LANGUAGE COMPREHENSION

BACKGROUND KNOWLEDGE
(facts, concepts, etc.)

VOCABULARY
(breadth, precision, links etc.)

LANGUAGE STRUCTURES
(syntax, semantics, etc.)

VERBAL REASONING
(inference, metaphor, etc.)

LITERACY KNOWLEDGE
(print concepts, genres, etc.)

WORD RECOGNITION

PHONOLOGICAL AWARENESS
(syllables, phonemes, etc.)

DECODING (alphabetic principle,
spelling-sound correspondences)

SIGHT RECOGNITION
(of familiar words)

increasingly strategic

increasingly automatic

SKILLED READING:
Fluent execution and coordination of word recognition and text comprehension.

Credit: Hollis Scarborough, "Connecting Early Language and Literacy to Later Reading (Dis)abilities: Evidence, Theory, and Practice" in *Handbook of Research in Early Literacy*, edited by Susan B. Neuman and David K. Dickinson © Guilford Press, 2001. Used with permission.

Both theoretical frameworks help educators understand the essential components that need to be part of instruction as students learn to read. Moving beyond these frameworks, a nuanced understanding of how the brain navigates print to master the reading process supports effective instruction. Numerous researchers have written about the phases of predictable reading development (Ehri 1995, Ehri and McCormick 1998, and Ehri and Snowling 2004). These phases, supported by instruction, provide readers with the ability to recognize words "by sight." The phases include the following:

- **Prealphabetic reading:** Reader uses a range of visual clues, such as a picture or a logo, to "read" words. Reader does not yet understand the letter-sound relationship.

- **Partial alphabetic reading and writing:** Reader uses some grapheme-phoneme, or letter-sound connections. This is known as *phonetic cue reading*. At this stage, the connections are not fully reliable.

- **Full alphabetic reading and writing:** Reader has basic sound/symbol correspondences and attends to every letter in every word. At this stage, readers can convert letters into sounds and words.

- **Consolidated alphabetic reading:** Reader has some sight vocabulary and a breadth of strategies to read unknown words. Reader uses chunks of words to support the reading of words.

- **Automatic reading:** Reader is skilled and recognizes most words. Unfamiliar words are approached with a variety of strategies.

Orthographic Mapping

Another term for how words are retrieved is *orthographic mapping*. The orthographic mapping process is how readers move from simple letter-sound correlation to phonetic decoding to the ability to quickly recognize words as part of a sight vocabulary. In orthographic mapping, readers use the oral language processing part of their brains to match phonemes (sounds within words) to the letters found inside words. As this mapping becomes more fluent, readers can instantly recognize words.

> " *Orthographic mapping* is the process readers use to store written words for immediate, effortless retrieval. It is the means by which readers turn unfamiliar words into familiar, instantaneously accessible sight words.
>
> —David A. Kilpatrick (2015, 81) "

Five Essential Components

Research continues in the field of education. In 2000, the National Reading Panel (NRP) published its review of studies to identify the components of effective reading instruction. This comprehensive report carefully examined a wide range of research. Within its narrative about how readers develop, the NRP's report articulated five essential components of reading:

- **Phonemic Awareness:** manipulating individual speech sounds

- **Phonics:** matching sounds to letters for use in reading and spelling

- **Fluency:** reading connected text accurately and fluently

- **Vocabulary:** knowing the meaning of words in speech and print
- **Reading Comprehension:** understanding what is read

Since the report was published, further research has only added to the body of research that supports the findings. The bottom line? Research continues to highlight the importance of integrated approaches to literacy instruction that include the five essential components in an intertwined way. Ultimately, the best ways to ensure students become engaged and successful readers and writers have not changed significantly.

This foundational information lays the groundwork for continued understanding of how to engage students with solid literacy instruction. Several institutions provide briefs or guides that present research in easily digestible formats. The Institute of Education Sciences/What Works Clearinghouse Practice Guides provide educators with sound instructional practices related to a range of literacy skills. Additionally, the International Literacy Association provides Leadership Briefs that highlight integral pedagogy with a strong research base.

The Focus on Writing

On the surface, the conversations tied to the Science of Reading do not address writing. The reality is that writing is incredibly important to the literacy achievement of students. Educators can turn to Scarborough's Reading Rope (2001) to easily see how the foundational components of reading instruction intricately align to the work of writing and the teaching of writing.

A careful examination quickly showcases the connections. For example, the strands of language comprehension, language structures, and verbal reasoning tie directly into writing instruction and the skills of grammar and mechanics.

> The writing process is one of the most powerful ways that students can showcase their understanding, communicate their learning, persuade others, and discover their voices.

Writing is important. "Writing is how students connect the dots in their knowledge" (National Commission on Writing 2003, 6). Without quality, science-based instruction in writing, literacy will continue to falter, and students will not develop the skills needed to be successful. Like reading, writing is complex. Learning to write requires a range of complex skills and immense practice.

Ultimately, writing instruction meets this purpose: "to construct real meaning" (Hawkins et al. 2008, 10).

The writing process is one of the most powerful ways that students can showcase their understanding, communicate their learning, persuade others, and discover their voices. There are many purposes for writing. Clearly connecting to the Science of Reading, teachers consistently ask students to write in response to reading. Students use writing to demonstrate their learning and the structures of language and text they have come across in their reading. Students are also asked to write to describe experiences, to provide reasoning for important action, to highlight their opinions, and to create original stories.

Primary teachers promote writing and support their students in various ways. Sentence frames provide students with structured and modeled experiences to help them put pencil to paper and highlight their voices. These experiences begin with simple options and pave the way for students to continue to develop the structures and knowledge that make them writers. Teachers infuse supports, such as graphic organizers and outlines, to help students put their ideas together. Teachers also use texts as models of great writing, further strengthening the connections between reading and writing.

Research consistently influences writing instruction. The Institute of Education Sciences (Graham et al. 2012, 2016) articulates key components to ensuring quality writing instruction. These components include the following:

Elementary Level

- Teach students the writing process.
  - ➤ Teach students strategies for the various components of the writing process.
  - ➤ Gradually release writing responsibility from the teacher to the student.
  - ➤ Guide students to select and use appropriate writing strategies.
  - ➤ Encourage students to be flexible in their use of the components of the writing process.
- Teach students to write for a variety of purposes.
  - ➤ Help students understand the different purposes of writing.
  - ➤ Expand students' concept of audience.

- ➤ Teach students to emulate the features of good writing.
- ➤ Teach students techniques for writing effectively for different purposes.

Secondary Level

- Use a Model-Practice-Reflect instructional cycle to teach writing strategies.
  - ➤ Model strategies for students.
  - ➤ Provide students with opportunities to apply and practice modeled strategies.

- Engage students in evaluating and reflecting upon their own and peers' writing and use of modeled strategies.

Joan Sedita (2019) developed a model that demonstrates the essential strands that contribute to skilled writing (see figure I.4). Sedita's Writing Rope is similar to the construct of the Reading Rope (Scarborough 2001). The strands include these five aspects of writing:

- **Critical Thinking:** Focus on critical thinking and executive functioning. Infuse awareness of the writing process and the use of background knowledge.
- **Syntax:** Focus on how sentences work.
- **Text Structure:** Focus on types of texts, paragraph structures, organizational patterns, and linking and transition words.
- **Writing Craft:** Focus on word choice, audience, and literary devices.
- **Transcription:** Focus on spelling, handwriting, and keyboarding skills.

Ultimately, the work of teaching writing is similarly complex to the teaching of reading and requires understanding the process of writing and how it works. The connections between reading and writing are immense and should regularly be made explicit to students. When students are engaged in reading complex and interesting texts, they are consistently exposed to the author's intentional decisions as a writer. Similarly, as students develop syntactical awareness through writing instruction, they develop rich understandings of how words work together to form meaning.

Figure I.4—Sedita's Writing Rope

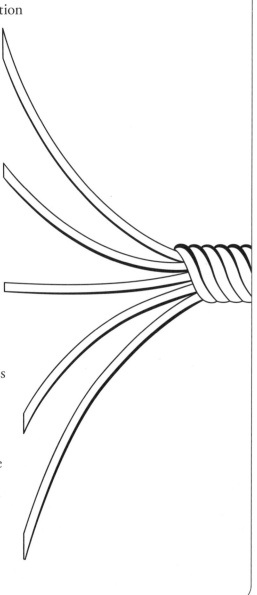

Critical Thinking

- Generating ideas, gathering information
- Writing process: organizing, drafting, writing, revising

Syntax

- Grammar and syntactic awareness
- Sentence elaboration
- Punctuation

Text Structure

- Narrative, informational, opinion structures
- Paragraph structure
- Patterns of organization (description, sequence, cause/effect, compare/contrast, problem/solution)
- Linking and transition words/phrases

Writing Craft

- Word choice
- Awareness of task, audience, purpose
- Literary devices

Transcription

- Spelling
- Handwriting, keyboarding

Credit: Sedita, J. 2019. "The Writing Rope: The Strands That Are Woven into Skilled Writing." Rowley, MA: Keys to Literacy. Used by permission.

Settled Science

When considering the body of research that is now known as the Science of Reading, there are implications for instruction that can be considered settled. David Kilpatrick (2015) notes, "We teach reading in different ways; [students] learn to read proficiently in only one way" (39). Recognizing that certain pedagogies and practices are settled science allows all educators to infuse them in their instruction. Instruction must be:

Evidence-based: Instruction and materials are anchored in trustworthy and reliable evidence. The evidence should demonstrate a consistent success record in increasing students' literacy abilities. Practices should build skills in phonemic awareness, phonics, vocabulary development, reading fluency (including oral-language skills), and reading comprehension.

Explicit: Instruction should include direct teaching that provides explanations of the concepts, modeling of the concepts, and practice with the concepts. Instruction should be clear, specific, and directly connected to an objective.

> " It is called *explicit* because it is an unambiguous and direct approach to teaching that includes both instructional design and delivery procedures. "
> —Anita Archer (2011, 1)

Systematic: Instruction should follow thoughtfully planned instructional routines. These routines should be planned in advance, ensuring maximum time on task.

Sequential: Instruction should teach skills and concepts sequentially from easiest to hardest. Foundational skills are taught to support higher-order skills. Sequencing should be intentional and within and across grades.

Rigorous for all: Instruction must include complex texts and tasks for all students. Referring to the practice of having students read only books at "their level," Sue Pimentel (2018) notes, "The texts they're reading don't require them to decipher unfamiliar vocabulary, confront challenging concepts, or parse new and complicated language" (para. 5). Every student needs opportunities to engage with difficult vocabulary, to build their knowledge and skills.

Intentional: Instruction should thoughtfully align to grade-level standards, and it should be scaffolded to support student needs. Assessment provides an understanding of what students know and what they need to know.

Engaging: Instruction should ensure students have a clear understanding of the objectives. It should enable students to make connections to their out-of-school lives and see the relevance of the work. Instruction should provide students with challenges and opportunities to take risks (Jackson and Zmuda 2014).

Designed to build knowledge: Instruction should be designed to build knowledge, vocabulary, and understanding about a range of topics. In a brief for the Knowledge Matters Campaign, Daniel Willingham notes, "Students need deep knowledge of a subject in order to think creatively or critically about it" (2016, 1).

Aligned to the essential components: Instruction must be aligned to the integral components of literacy instruction as indicated by the evidence. It should focus on the five essential components showcased by the National Reading Panel (2000). Written expression (composition) and oral language (speaking and listening) are also essential components of literacy.

From the Classroom

Bubble Trouble
by Janea

Let me tell you how to blow a bubble. Get a piece of gum. Unwrap your gum. Throw the wrapper away. Put your gum in your mouth. Chew your gum to get the sugar out of it. Flatten the gum against your teeth. Stick your tongue into the gum. Blow hard! Now you know how to blow a bubble.

As you read this student's writing example, did you want to grab some bubble gum and discover if the directions lead you to blow a great bubble? I blew the best bubble after reading these directions! Full disclosure: I admit, there is a chance that I filled in the missing pieces. I know the author. I love the author. (She is my daughter.) Other readers would likely find some shortcomings in this writing. Given that she was a young writer, there are a lot of great things going on in this little paragraph.

- The writer uses complete sentences.
- The writer introduces the topic and provides a closing.
- The writer uses a variety of punctuation to support meaning.
- The writer uses a range of vocabulary to show detail.

There are some things missing, too.

- The writer did not use time-order words.
- The writer did not vary sentence structure.

This experience provided my daughter with an opportunity to put pencil to paper. It was one of many writing opportunities her first-grade teacher provided. Student samples such as this give teachers information about what students can do and what they need to learn how to do. In this book, we share how to analyze the skills proficient writers need, and provide effective writing instruction.

—Jen Jump

Navigating This Book

Each of the first five chapters of this book showcases important research that supports the instruction of writing across the content areas.

Chapter 1	The Recursive Writing Process
Chapter 2	Genre Characteristics
Chapter 3	Prewriting and Organization
Chapter 4	Revise for Purpose: Syntax of Sentences and Beyond
Chapter 5	Grammar, Usage, and Mechanics

These chapters are structured to bridge the gap between the science of literacy instruction and classroom practice. Each chapter begins by examining the research with a thoughtful and critical eye. Following the research, you will find instructional implications. These implications identify how the research should impact the work of educators in classrooms today. Next, you will find key terms for teacher understanding. Each of these key terms is defined and showcased in a classroom example.

Each chapter also includes research-based instructional strategies. These strategies are aligned to grade-level bands: K–1, 2–3, 4–5, and secondary. However, many of these strategies have utility across grade levels and can be modified to support students beyond the bands suggested. Each chapter closes with the following sections:

- **Top Must-Dos:** A summary of research implications, the must-do list supports all teachers as they navigate taking the Science of Reading directly into their classrooms.

- **Further Considerations:** Offering additional insights about effective instruction, this section also includes (as appropriate) guidance for moving away from practices that are not supported by research.

- **Reflection Questions:** A short list of questions to push the practice of engaged educators provides conversation starters for professional learning or self-reflection.

The final chapter in this book, written by guest author Kim Carlton, takes an in-depth look at an effective strategy every teacher should be using—micro writing. Ms. Carlton demonstrates the power of this strategy for ensuring that students experience small wins that lead to big wins in their writing.

Take a deep breath. While we educators do not have a Hippocratic oath, we know the great responsibility we face each day. Louisa Moats (2020) said it best: "Teaching reading is rocket science." Let's build the literacy rocket together.

Chapter 1

The Recursive Writing Process

Background Information and Research

As much as teachers struggle to help students learn to read, they often struggle more helping students learn to write. Reading may be seen as a skill, or set of skills, that can be practiced and taught, but writing is often seen as an inherent talent or gift. Moreover, teachers are generally confident readers, so they know what good reading looks like. And while they may recognize good writing, they may not be confident writers themselves, and so they feel insecure judging the writing of another or knowing the right strategy to use to help a growing writer. Also important to remember—writing is not an automatic extension of speaking. "When we write, we don't have visual cues to draw on, and we often don't know exactly who the audience is. We need to express ourselves with far more precision and clarity, anticipating the facts and details a reader will require to grasp our meaning. We also need to rely on words and punctuation rather than intonation and pauses to indicate nuances in meaning or breaks in the narrative" (Hochman and Wexler 2017, 34).

> When students learn to write, they are learning how to approach reading from a new and enlarged perspective.

Learning to read *does* rely on a set of skills, and writing does as well. Writing is inextricably tied to reading because behind everything you read is a *writer* who made decisions about how to put those words together. "Readers apply what they know about the functions and purposes of written language to help them interpret an author's message. Writers draw on this same knowledge to help them construct their own text for others to read" (International Literacy Association 2020, 4). Learning to write is like going backstage at a show, seeing how everything works, how it all is organized, planned out, and presented. When students learn to write, they are learning how to approach reading from a new and enlarged perspective. Similarly, the more practice students have with reading, the more examples they have to draw upon for their own writing. It is on the teacher to make the connection by pointing out the specific characteristics of a text and the specific choices the author made. "[W]hen teachers guide students in the analysis of mentor texts, students better understand the purposes and construction of specific genres" (International Literacy Association 2020, 2).

Connection to the Ropes

The Reading Rope (Scarborough 2001) describes the process of learning to read as resembling strands of a rope, each strand representing one component of the process, woven together to symbolize the interconnectedness of each component. Some of the components become more automatic for students as they gain more practice; some of the components become more strategic, and students must up the metacognitive ante to access more complex text.

In much the same way, the writing process is a combination of multiple skills. Joan Sedita's Writing Rope (figure I.4) describes the strands of critical thinking, syntax, text structure, writing craft, and transcription. Students think critically about ideas and information and the stages of the writing process. As they draft, they use their understanding of grammar and elaboration to craft their sentences. They pay attention to text structures as they organize their ideas and make choices about appropriate transition words. These decisions are driven by their awareness of task, audience, and purpose, which also informs their language choices and tone. The final strand includes the finishing touches, the spelling and the formatting of the text.

Sedita states "Instruction for many skills that support writing also support reading comprehension" (2019, 1). As students become more proficient readers, they will start to judge their own writing from a readers' perspective, which will in turn help them improve their writing.

Research supports giving students multiple opportunities to practice writing. The goal is to make them comfortable with writing and to show them how to continually perfect their work. "As students write, they learn by doing. They try out different forms of writing, apply different strategies and approaches for producing text, and gain fluency with basic writing skills such as handwriting, spelling, and sentence construction" (International Literacy Association 2020, 3).

Practice can take many forms, from responding to questions, taking notes, drafting quick-writes, composing journal entries, or writing short narratives.

Younger students should spend about 30 minutes each day writing. Older students should also spend time writing regularly and use writing as a tool for learning (Graham et al. 2012).

Implications for Teaching and Learning

As student writing endurance increases, teachers can call attention to the writing process itself. There are distinct stages to effective writing: prewriting or planning, drafting, revising, editing, and publishing (see Key Terms for Teacher Understanding on pages 25–26). Prewriting or planning is the time when students can brainstorm, try out ideas, gather research and evidence, and basically do all the preliminary work before actually starting to write. Prewriting and planning may be hard to evaluate, as students often get ideas outside of the classroom. Thinking and planning are not always visible, but when time is devoted to this stage of the process, students come to see the value of think-time. Encourage students to track their thinking in a journal so they can reference their ideas later.

> " As students write, they learn by doing. They try out different forms of writing, apply different strategies and approaches for producing text, and gain fluency with basic writing skills such as handwriting, spelling, and sentence construction. "
>
> —International Literacy Association (2020, 3)

At this point, students may feel ready to write and dive in with vigor. It can be challenging to convince students to revisit their work when they have expended so much energy in their drafts. So before drafting, have students organize their prewriting, using color-coding or sticky notes. This allows them to move their thoughts around before committing them to paper. Remind them they are just trying things out at this point, so they do not need to worry about "perfection." There will be time devoted to revising drafts and editing. Drafting comes next, when students use their organized ideas to write. Whether they are creating sentences, paragraphs, or pages, drafting is an important step.

Revision "involves making content changes after students first have evaluated problems within their text that obscure their intended meaning. Students should make changes to clarify or enhance their meaning. These changes may include reorganizing their ideas, adding or removing whole sections of text, and refining their word choice and sentence structure" (Graham et al. 2012, 14). This is where the planning process becomes relevant again, as students can revisit their notes, reorganize, and rewrite. Using online tools lets them save multiple versions of their work, which may be valuable if they decide to reinsert something they had previously cut out. Great topic sentences, interesting descriptions, or other creative turns of phrase may not fit in the assignment at hand, but students should be encouraged to save these gems—they may be just right for another assignment!

More precision is used during the editing stage, when students look for specific details to address, such as conventions, grammar, spelling, punctuation, and overall appearance. Much like cleaning your room before company arrives, editing is the final clean-up to make an impressive product for the reader. Checklists and mnemonics help students remember to look at each component carefully.

Once the revisions and edits are complete, students publish their work, which simply means prepare it for public view, as an oral presentation, a beautifully printed document, or a multi-media piece with art and text. It is not necessary to publish every piece of writing, but students should experience this final stage with some writing assignments so they can take pride in their hard work. Have students keep writing portfolios and select their favorite pieces to publish and display.

Research confirms that students need strategies to successfully engage in each of these stages. They need modeling and explicit instruction, with a gradual release of responsibility to boost their confidence and foster perseverance. "When students are taught how to engage in the process of writing, their compositions become longer, full, and qualitatively better" (International Literacy Association 2020, 6). In studies where teachers devoted considerable time to writing instruction, their use of evidence-based practices promoted writing success and growth. These practices included "writing for different purposes, teaching strategies for carrying out writing processes…and teaching students foundational writing skills like handwriting, spelling, and sentence construction" (Graham 2019, 279).

It is important to remember that the writing process does not necessarily happen in a particular order. Writers may move fluidly between stages—backward, forward, and even skipping or repeating stages. "Writing is not a linear process, like following a recipe to bake a cake. It is flexible; writers should learn to move easily back and forth between components of the writing process, often altering their plans and revising their text along the way" (Graham et al. 2012, 14).

Key Terms for Teacher Understanding

The following chart provides definitions of essential terms educators need to know and an example of each one.

Term and Definition	Example
drafting—the stage of the writing process when a preliminary version of text is created	Juan has recorded all the steps of a science experiment. He needs to write a description of the experiment, including the outcome. Juan uses his notes to roughly explain the sequence of events step-by-step. He tries to use complete sentences, but sometimes he abbreviates terms, or he uses bullet points, drawings, or shorthand, knowing that he will return to the draft later for revision.
editing—the stage of the writing process when changes are made to ensure the writing adheres to the conventions of written English, including grammar, spelling, word choice, punctuation, and formatting	Lamar's first draft of his report is complete. He has reviewed the writing to make sure the ideas are clear. Now, he returns to his draft one more time to make sure that he has capitalized all the proper nouns, used the appropriate punctuation, and spelled everything correctly. His teacher gave him a way to remember how to edit, using the mnemonic device COPS to remind himself to check *capitalization*, *overall* appearance, *punctuation*, and *spelling*.
prewriting—the stage of the writing process when writers develop goals, generate ideas, gather information, organize ideas, and develop a logical structure	Vi is asked to write a response to a question about a character in a book he is reading: "Why was the character suspicious?" Vi uses a timeline to recall the events of the story. He rereads several pages of the story to find evidence that the character was suspicious. He records examples of how the character was suspicious using a three-column chart to note the page, the quote, and his analysis of the quote. When he has two or three good examples, he begins planning how he will organize them in response to the question.

(Continued)

Term and Definition	Example
publication—a final product that is shared in written and/or oral form	Each student in Mr. Johnson's class writes something about their family as a get-to-know-you activity. Mr. Johnson asks each student to create a picture that represents their family and to include it with the written description. Students record themselves reading the stories and link the recordings through QR codes printed on the pictures. The finished stories and pictures are posted around the room, and parents use their cell phones to listen to their children read the stories during back-to-school night.
recursive—a process that is looped so that it is repeated and revisited	Xochitl is assigned a research project. She has an idea that she jots down in her notebook so she can remember it. Later that day, she returns to her notebook to flesh out the thought. As she is elaborating on her first idea, she realizes she needs more information, so she stops writing and begins researching. Her research leads her to revise the original idea. As she is revising, she notices that she has used the same transition word three times already, so she begins editing by replacing two of the transition words with other choices. Then, she returns to her research, takes some more notes, and adds some information to her draft.
revision—the stage of the writing process when the author reviews, alters, and amends the content of writing by adding, deleting, or rearranging to clarify or enhance meaning	Kendra wrote a draft narrative about a time she overcame a fear. Her classmate read it and had questions about the events in the story. Kendra reread her narrative and realized she had not been clear about some of the events. She returns to the story to add a little more detail and to make sure that the cause-and-effect relationships of the events are more evident by adding cue words and by reordering them.

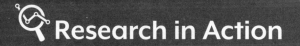

Draw, Write, Edit

Grades: K–1

Description

Draw, Write, Edit is an introduction to the writing process for young students. Students draw pictures in response to prompts. Students may add descriptions or captions to the pictures in their own words and invented spellings. Students use a clear editing checklist to make edits to their drawings.

Rationale

Draw, Write, Edit shows students that they can return to an assignment and make adjustments or edits to improve the product. Introducing editing at this stage allows students to learn this skill in an authentic context rather than as an isolated activity, and gives them permission to revisit work to make it better.

Roles and Responsibilities

Teacher: Facilitator

- Provides a model and thinks aloud through the process of creating the drawing, including adding a caption.

- Asks specific students to share what they are considering drawing (**planning**).

- Emphasizes that students will first **draft** their drawings in pencil, and that they will have an opportunity to revisit their drawings (**edit**) before finalizing them (**publishing**).

- Provides explicit editing checklists so students purposefully return to the work.

Student: Author and artist

- Brainstorms ideas with partners or in table groups.

- Practices sentences orally before writing.

- Uses the checklist with a partner to peer edit each other's drawings and then makes the recommended edits.

Process

1. Develop an editing checklist for the drawing, such as:

   - Did I include lots of details?
   - Did I use the whole page?
   - Did I add writing?

2. Ask students to respond to a prompt or question, such as "What is your favorite animal?" or "What is your morning routine before school?"

3. Model by creating a draft drawing, and then orally describe what was drawn, pointing out specific details and other elements on the editing checklist.

4. Have students create their drawings using pencils and then work with partners to describe their drawings orally.

5. Introduce the editing checklist, and model how to check the drawing. Ask students to provide feedback on the draft picture for each element on the checklist.

6. Have students work with partners to check each other's writing. Monitor as students edit their own drawings.

Differentiation

Provide shapes or patterns as templates as students begin to sketch. Keep the editing checklist on a table tent for reference. Have students describe their drawings as they practice invented spelling, or let students use an app to record their descriptions orally.

Lists

Grades: 2–3

Description

This is a prewriting strategy to help students organize and plan for writing. Students generate multiple ideas and then categorize the information. Sorting ideas in this way helps students prepare for the drafting stage of the writing process.

Rationale

Brainstorming is often a futile effort if students do not feel they know enough about a topic. This prewriting strategy provides specific guidance by asking students to come up with at least five detail words. Providing criteria encourages discussion and perseverance and may spark new connections.

Roles and Responsibilities

Teacher: Recorder

- Records information shared by students.
- Provides a graphic organizer for setting up lists.
- Validates different ways that students organize their lists.
- Encourages continued use of lists through mini-lessons and prewriting activities.

Student: Creative thinker

- Brainstorms ideas with partners or in table groups.
- Makes connections and justifies thinking.

Process

1. Introduce a topic, and ask students to generate lists of words related to the topic. Write one word per sticky note, and post the words on chart paper or on the board. Some topic examples include:

    *   pets
    *   family
    *   seasons
    *   your neighborhood

2. Have students work with partners or in small groups. Assign new topics, and have students work together to generate lists using sticky notes and chart paper.

3. Ask students to do a gallery walk and then return to their own lists to see if there are any words they would like to add or change.

4. Ask students to explain the connections between the words in the list and the topic.

Differentiation

Display pictures or photos with the topics to help generate ideas. As students are explaining the connections between words on their lists, write what they say on chart paper and post it. To narrow students' focus, assign criteria to each set of lists, such as "sensory words" or "feeling words." Students can also create lists digitally, and insert photos or pictures.

Revise or Edit?

Description

Students differentiate between actions they take with their writing, determining if they are revisions or edits. This activity helps students recognize the difference between reading a draft for content and reading a draft for mechanics.

Rationale

Writing is never one-and-done. Starting a habit of revisiting writing encourages thoughtful reflection and shows students the value of continuously improving their work. Each stage is a separate part of the writing process and requires a different critical eye. Addressing content and mechanics separately emphasizes the importance of each stage.

Roles and Responsibilities

Teacher: Facilitator

- Provides models of writing, either from mentor texts or from other students.

- Creates a criteria checklist to distinguish content revisions from edits.

- Thinks aloud and models the process using annotations and proofreading marks.

Student: Editor

- Works with partners or in small groups to make decisions about revising and editing.

- Uses and understands annotations and proofreading marks.

Process

1. On a sheet of chart paper, define *revision* as an opportunity to reorganize content, provide clarification, or modify language choices.

2. Create a checklist that includes questions such as:

   - Does the writing flow logically?
   - Are the details clear?
   - Have the best words been used?

3. On another sheet of chart paper, define *edit* as an opportunity to check for mechanics such as punctuation, grammar, spelling, and formatting.

4. Create a checklist that includes questions such as:

   - Are all the sentences capitalized? Do they all have end punctuation?
   - Are quotes used correctly?
   - Are all the verbs the same tense? Do singular and plural nouns have matching verbs?
   - Are there spelling mistakes?
   - Does the writing look neat and fit on the line?

5. Include proofreader's marks for "insert," "delete," and "capitalize."

6. Introduce a model paragraph that has both content and mechanical errors. Think aloud and demonstrate how to use each checklist by using one color marker to highlight and make revisions and a different color to highlight and make edits. Use the correct proofreader's marks.

7. Give each student two colored markers. Have them exchange papers with a partner. In the first round, have students use the checklist to look for and highlight revisions. In the next round, have students use the checklist to look for and highlight edits.

8. Have students explain their markings to their partners, with suggestions for how to address the changes.

Differentiation

- Play a game by having students examine sentences and identify one revision and one edit.

- Laminate copies of the criteria checklists, and have students keep them at their desks for reference.

- Have students use highlighting tools on digital documents to call out revisions for peer editing. Have them use the Comment tool to insert edits.

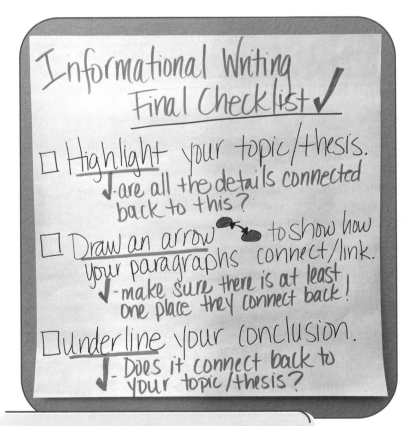

Informational Writing
Final Checklist ✔

☐ Highlight your topic/thesis.
   ✔ -are all the details connected back to this?

☐ Draw an arrow to show how your paragraphs connect/link.
   ✔ -make sure there is at least one place they connect back!

☐ underline your conclusion.
   ✔ - Does it connect back to your topic/thesis?

Students use this three-point checklist to support the revision process when writing informational text.

Talk First, Write Next

Secondary Grades

Description

Talk First, Write Next helps students rehearse what they want to say before they commit their ideas to paper. Students draft their responses orally first and get verbal feedback from their peers. This shared conversation seeds their writing.

Rationale

Exchanging ideas with peers lets students audition their thoughts and gives them a chance to practice using academic and content-specific language. For English learners, the chance to listen and to speak is a crucial launch point for writing.

Roles and Responsibilities

Teacher: Facilitator

- Provides structured time for students to share their thoughts orally before drafting.

- Models how to ask questions and how to respond using complete sentences.

Student: Interviewer and Recorder

- Asks targeted questions about writing.

- Responds orally before beginning to draft.

Process

1. Students work in small groups or pairs to discuss writing prior to putting pencil to paper.

2. Provide a topic—something they have been studying or a response to something they are reading.

3. Use starter questions, such as:

   - What details support your theme?

   - Will you use any figurative language? How will it help the reader?

- What words are important to include?

- What is the structure you will use?

- Are there any details you know you need to include?

4. After students have had time to discuss their ideas, have them begin to organize their thoughts and start writing. Remind them to use academic and content-specific vocabulary.

Differentiation

- Create a question bank, and let students add their own questions.

- Provide sentence stems to help students turn their oral responses into written responses.

- Show students a word bank with academic and content-specific vocabulary to include in their responses.

- **Mathematics:** Remind students to identify the components of the problem and describe how it will be solved, using a step-by-step structure; include transition words in their word banks.

- **Science:** Have students identify a Science and Engineering Practice or Cross-Cutting Concept in their responses.

- **Social Studies:** Tell students to each reference a source in their responses, using a citation or a quote.

Moving Forward: Top Must-Dos

As Steve Graham and his colleagues explain, "Teachers need to explicitly instruct students on writing strategies and how to select the most appropriate strategy. Eventually, as students become experienced writers, they will use these strategies automatically to write effectively" (2016, 7).

Provide Instruction for Brainstorming and Revising

Brainstorming does not have to be unstructured. In fact, the freedom to write anything can be intimidating for those who are less confident. Providing structures and explicit criteria can foster creativity. For example, instead of asking students to brainstorm how to support an idea with details, provide specific types of details they will be expected to use, such as "details that explain why," or "details that describe external characteristics." Provide sentence starters and transition words to spur their thinking.

The same process can be used for revision. Students can easily fall into writing patterns, using strings of simple sentences. These get tedious for the reader who craves intonation and variety to keep the reading interesting. Give students rules and restrictions as they revise. For instance, have them circle all the sentences that start with the word *the*. Challenge them to change half of those to start with verbs. Work with them to generate a long list of sequence words, such as *first*, *next*, *then*, and so on. Tell them they must not repeat any of these words in a paragraph. Or assign vocabulary words monetary values—ten-cent words are simple, fifty-cent words are a little more complex, and five-dollar words are highly academic. Have them work with partners to increase the dollar values of their writing.

Provide Structures for Writing

Graphic organizers are tools that help students organize their thinking. Bubble-maps, T-charts, time lines, three-column charts, even handprints used to remember the five *Ws* (*who, what, where, when, why*)—all these can help put ideas into an organized structure. As students learn about genres, text structure becomes more relevant to the writing process. Problem-solution structures, for example, are used for expository text in social studies. Students can start organizing their thinking by listing problems on one side of a page, with lines drawn to historical solutions. Using strategies to put their thoughts in order is a transferable skill that will serve them in secondary grades and across content areas.

Folded paper organizers, interactive notebooks, or even online tools can support structures to guide writing. Remember that the outcome is not the creation of a perfect graphic organizer. The graphic organizer should be a tool that is useful for the student. The goal is for the student to learn how to find and use resources to help them in the future.

Sentence stems demonstrate the minimum expectation for speaking and writing. In secondary grades, teachers may have concerns that stems are too much of a scaffold, but on the contrary, showing students exemplar models elevates their thinking and gets them in the habit of responding using complete and complex sentences. Keep sentence stems posted around the room or on table tents, and have students contribute ideas and examples. Require students to always respond orally using complete sentences, with the stems as the models. It may seem forced at first, but these tools are especially helpful for English learners or striving readers, many of whom might never have experienced the successful completion of a well-written paragraph.

Text structures represent categories of text types or genres. Structures can be sequential, like lists or process steps, or they can be temporal, like a series of events. Narrative structures might include flashbacks, and persuasive structures might present one side of an issue in the first paragraph and a contrary view in the next. Help students recognize the structures by looking at the transition words. If they see words like *first*, *next*, and *finally*, what kind of structure are they most likely reading? Go a little deeper and ask, "Why do authors choose a particular structure?" Lists are helpful for remembering instructions; narrative story structures build tension and suspense leading to a climax. Tell students these transition words are clues for the reader to help understand the motivation of the author.

Support Students with Editing and Revising Guidelines

Clearly defined criteria for formatting, conventions, and mechanics will reinforce the importance of these finishing touches. Just like the accessories one adds to an outfit, tiny details can enhance a piece of writing. Attention paid to these criteria demonstrates pride in the work and tells the reader that care was taken in creating this piece. Use mentor texts and student exemplars as models, and walk students through the editing process one step at a time.

- **Checklists:** Keep it simple at first, editing for three or four specific conventions. Students can peer edit each other's work and use the checklists to help direct their partners' work and ultimately their own work as well. Expand the process using color-coding for different types of conventions, including grammar, spelling, or punctuation. Teach students annotation tools so they can call attention to places where the writing is confusing or where they have specific questions.

- **Rubrics:** An extension of the checklist is the rubric, which sets a goal and also provides information about growth. A rubric provides clear guidelines about what is expected to earn 2 out of 4 points, versus what is expected to earn 3 out of 4 points. A rubric outlines exactly what is needed to improve the product so students can set and achieve goals. Going through the rubric before the writing project begins lets the student know the expectations and reinforces the idea that writing is a process that takes time and attention.

Further Considerations

Provide Explicit Prompts

Writing instruction relies on explicit writing prompts that clearly identify what the student is expected to do. Model the importance of clarity by being explicit yourself. We take for granted that our students understand what we are asking them to do, but students may be too shy or unsure to ask for clarification. Run your assignments by a colleague or an instructional coach, and ask if they understand your expectations. Sometimes, it is helpful to complete your own assignment as if you were a student. As you create a model, you may see where students will get stuck or have questions. Use that knowledge to revisit your prompt to see how to prevent those questions from arising, and maintain a safe environment where students feel comfortable asking for help.

Model Risk and Release Responsibility

Be willing to take risks, allowing time to model and demonstrate and release responsibility to students. The gradual release model serves the teacher by making student thinking visible. Build in checkpoints to stop and confirm that students are understanding what to do and how to do it. Redirect their thinking while their conceptual understanding is still malleable. Once a mistake is embedded in a student's thinking, it will take much longer to undo. Better to spend that time at the front end of the process.

Provide Time to Talk before Writing

Build in time for students to talk before they are asked to write. Rehearsal is the key to a good performance. When students get a chance to try out their ideas orally first, they get to practice with academic language, they get to hear novel sentence constructions, and they are exposed to different expressions of thought. Pair English learners with more fluent speakers who can serve as language brokers, gently nudging them toward language proficiency. Encourage students to use the language from their conversations in their writing.

My Teaching Checklist

Are you ready to develop students' understanding of the stages of the writing process? Use this checklist to help you get started!

The Recursive Writing Process

Look Fors	Description
Students have opportunities for engagement in all steps of the process.	• Only teach one stage of the writing process at a time. • Provide explicit instructions. • Give opportunities to revisit every stage of the process.
The gradual release model is used.	• Model and think aloud. • Provide examples and non-examples as mentor text. • Include intentional check-ins to stop and monitor students.
Students' sense of ownership is promoted.	• Keep portfolios of student work. • Celebrate writing by publishing and displaying work.

Chapter Summary

Reading and writing are interconnected skills. As students become more proficient readers, they are also filling their writing toolboxes with great examples of language choices, text structures, and complex sentences. While highlighting reading and comprehension strategies, discuss the tools used by the writer to hold the interest of the reader. Show students that writing well is not some mysterious gift; it is a set of skills that can be learned, practiced, and perfected. Introduce the writing process, and explicitly teach students strategies for addressing each stage. Foster flexibility by stressing the recursive nature of writing, and remind students that writing is not necessarily a linear process. They may move back and forth through the writing process as they reflect and refine their writing. Remember that students need to rehearse their ideas by speaking and listening before they start to write and that they need to return to their writing multiple times to revise and edit. Give students many opportunities to write so they gain confidence and feel comfortable with writing.

Reflection Questions

- What is your writing process? Are you a confident writer? How does this affect your instruction?

- In what ways do you include writing in your instruction?

- What opportunities do students have to write for fun?

- What are some structured opportunities you provide for students to practice speaking and listening?

- How do you support the recursive writing process?

Chapter 2

Genre Characteristics

From the Classroom

To infuse creativity into the curriculum, I often use writing. One of my favorite examples was a creative writing unit involving the "Little Miss" and "Mr. Men" book series by Roger Hargreaves. Each book was a small square that young children could easily hold and navigate. It told the story of a single character, such as "Mr. Messy" or "Little Miss Brave," and often talked about the characteristics of each one and often how they evolved. We read many of these books in class before the students wrote stories of their own. Then, they each chose an adjective for their character and created a story plan for how their character would change.

One student titled his story "Mr. Wild." As I was conferring with him one day, I casually asked him how he had chosen that adjective. He answered quite simply, "Well, I think I'm a little wild sometimes, and I don't know how to control myself." I was speechless. It was through this character that this boy was actually writing about himself. In writing his story, he had to think of some strategies to help his character become "a little more relaxed," and ultimately, was helping himself learn how to do this.

It is through creative writing that children learn to express the deepest parts of themselves that otherwise might have never been brought to the forefront. To me, creative writing isn't just something that links to a standard. In an age of high emphasis on social-emotional learning, it is a necessity, not only to develop writing skills, but also to truly understand our students, and ultimately, help them to understand themselves.

—Amy Sroka, Former Fourth Grade Teacher
The Leffell School
White Plains, New York

Background Information and Research

Writing serves many purposes. First and foremost, it is a communication tool. It is a way for people to advocate for themselves, to express their ideas, to share their feelings. "In today's increasingly diverse society, writing is a gateway for success in academia, the new workplace, and the global economy, as well as for our collective success as a participatory democracy" (National Writing Project and Carl Nagin 2006, 2).

The most important quality of good writing is its comprehensibility. If the communication is not clear, the writer has not been successful. This is true whether writing for school, writing to get a job, writing to instruct, or writing to entertain. "In the business world, as well as in school, students must convey complex ideas and information in a clear, succinct manner. Inadequate writing skills…could inhibit achievement…while proficient writing skills help students convey ideas, deliver instructions, analyze information, and motivate others" (U.S. Department of Education 1998, 70). And in the modern world, writing is now embedded in technology tools—texts, emails, and social media have made writing ubiquitous, and therefore it is more important than ever to write with accuracy and precision.

> " In today's increasingly diverse society, writing is a gateway for success in academia, the new workplace, and the global economy, as well as for our collective success as a participatory democracy.
>
> —National Writing Project and Carl Nagin (2006, 2) "

Writing can be categorized into types, called *genres*. Identifying the genre provides a roadmap for the writer, with common organizational structures and features. Like a pattern for sewing or a template for painting, the genre is the form that supports the function of the art. "When students understand writing as a genre…they will not only write more effectively…but will also acquire the tools they need to address new writing situations" (Clark and Hernandez 2011, 65). Overarching genres include narrative, expository, and persuasive writing. Within these genres are more nuanced versions, such as informative or descriptive writing. Each genre has a set of generalizable rules. Narratives tell stories, and their structure is often linear, but could also include flashbacks or be told from two points of view. Expository writing is typically nonfiction and explanatory or informational. News articles, reports, and essays are examples of informational writing. Persuasive writing is argumentative, stating a claim and using evidence to convince or prove. It can take the form of an editorial, a review, a report, a speech, or a letter. Students at any grade level can write within any genre. For grades K–2, they can write opinions about their favorite foods. Students in grades 3–6 can argue why homework should be abolished. Secondary students can tackle a social justice issue with a persuasive letter to the school newspaper. As students become more familiar with genres, more skilled at reading comprehension strategies, and more comfortable as writers, they will improve the way they support their ideas, the ways they organize their thoughts, and the choices they make about language and sentence structure.

Connection to the Ropes

In Scarborough's Reading Rope (2001), comprehension is dependent upon background knowledge, an understanding of vocabulary, language structures, verbal reasoning, and literacy knowledge, including genre. These complex and multifaceted strands are woven together with the more automatic components of reading, such as word recognition and decoding. As students engage with more complex texts, they need strategies that will help them unpack meaning. One of the strategies is an understanding of genre. Recognizing genre as a means of sorting text types helps students be more discerning readers. They will approach text with a basic expectation of finding specific features. As writers, students can transfer the features that they read into expressions that they include when they write.

Readers can start to recognize vocabulary and language structures as clues to the genre. As they read, are they noticing a problem-and-solution structure? This might be a persuasive text. Did they pick up on the use of clear character descriptions? They may be reading a narrative. Is the text giving them data and statistics? Chances are this writing is trying to inform and instruct.

> Recognizing genre as a means of sorting text types helps students be more discerning readers. They will approach text with a basic expectation of finding specific features.

Similarly, Sedita's Writing Rope (2019) weaves together strategic processes and automatic processes. Strategically, when students write, they use genre to make choices about composition. They use their knowledge of form to make word choices. They structure their sentences and order their ideas to give clear direction to the reader about the genre so the reader knows what to expect and what to look for. "Students engage in critical thinking as they think about what they want to communicate through their writing" (Sedita 2019, 1). Each time they make a conscious and intentional decision about their writing, they are improving their writing proficiency.

Implications for Teaching and Learning

"Text structure is unique to written language, and awareness of several levels of text structure supports both writing and reading comprehension. Students benefit from explicit instruction in several levels of text structure" (Sedita 2019, 2). Teaching genres explicitly provides a foundation for students' reading comprehension. Teaching about the *idea* of genre lets students understand that text functions in diverse ways. "Explicit teaching of a genre may enable students to replicate that genre; fostering genre 'awareness' enables students to gain a 'threshold concept'" (Clark and Hernandez 2011, 67).

Writing revolves around three key components: task, audience, and purpose. These three elements work together to determine the structure of the writing, the language used, the tone, and even the types of details and descriptions to include. Across all grade levels, students are asked to understand task, audience, and purpose when they write. The *task* represents the form of the writing: a letter, an essay, an email, a brochure, or a research report. Each form has a different set of rules about format, length, and style. For younger students, introductory writing tasks could be a drawing or one sentence, while older students might be asked to write a complex set of instructions or a lengthy lab report.

> Writing revolves around three key components: task, audience, and purpose. These three elements work together to determine the structure of the writing, the language used, the tone, and even the types of details and descriptions to include.

Audience represents who will be receiving the message you are trying to convey. The first rule of writing is "know your audience." The audience dictates the language choices, the tone, and the structure of the writing. A letter to your friend will have a casual tone and use less formal language than a letter to a prospective employer. Sometimes, students will be writing to their peers or pen pals. Other times, the audience may be their teachers, or students may be reaching a broader audience such as community members, newspapers, or college admissions offices.

Finally, the *purpose* of the writing represents the *why*—What is the writing meant to achieve? Is the purpose to inform, explain, entertain, or convince? The purpose will be achieved by the organization of the ideas and by the types of details, evidence, and background information included. If trying to persuade, words may be chosen to provide evidence that plays on emotion, or data that supports credibility. If trying to entertain, the details should evoke sensory connections or perhaps strike a comic tone. If using writing to instruct, clear and descriptive terms and step-by-step procedures may be most effective. For early grades, it is important to be explicit about the purpose of the writing. Older students may be able to address nuances of purpose, like propaganda as an extension of persuasion or unreliable narrators in storytelling.

Key Terms for Teacher Understanding

The following chart provides definitions of essential terms educators need to know and an example of each one.

Term and Definition	Example
argument—the key to an opinion, the argument is comprised of all the pieces that support the opinion and ultimately persuade others to share the opinion	Krystal thinks it is unfair that only four students are allowed at each lunch table. She wants to sit with more of her friends. The teacher suggests Krystal write an argument, in which she presents her opinion, provides her reasons, and addresses the concerns of the teacher (Will more students be too noisy and too messy?). Krystal works with her friends to put together an argument, and they all make a presentation to the teacher.

(Continued)

Term and Definition	Example
characters—people, animals, beings, creatures, or things in a story; the characters perform the actions and speak the dialogue that make the story progress	After reading the poem "Where I'm From" by George Ella Lyon, Mr. Nguyen asks students to describe the character in the poem. Students discuss what they learned and what they inferred about the character, citing lines from the poem. Next, Mr. Nguyen tells students to write "I Am From" poems, which will be their personal character sketches. He provides sentence stems that mirror the structure of the poem he read aloud. He tells students the stems are a guide to help them include a description of how they look, where they live, who their friends are, something about their families, and a saying or motto that defines them. After students are done writing, Mr. Nguyen reads one or two aloud each day, without giving the name, and asks the other students to guess whom the poem is about. Later, as the students read other stories, Mr. Nguyen asks them to write "I Am From" poems about some of the characters.
claims/counterclaims—claims are arguments; counterclaims are opposing arguments	The ninth-grade English class is reading *Julius Caesar*. The teacher asks students which character did the most harm—Brutus or Cassius. After giving them a moment to think, she asks the students to go to different corners of the room based on which character they chose. Students discuss their opinions. Then, one student from the Brutus group presents their claim. A student from the Cassius group presents a counterclaim. Both groups use representatives to continue the discussion and present opposing points of view, using evidence from the play. Then, the teacher asks them all to write paragraphs on this topic.

Term and Definition	Example
evidence (support)—facts, documentation, or testimony used to strengthen a claim, support an argument, or reach a conclusion	In science, students are each given a rubber ball and a paper clip. They are asked to prove that both the ball and the paper clip will fall to the ground at the same rate. Working with partners, students gather evidence by dropping both from the same height. Then, they use the textbook to research the formulas for speed and velocity. They use the evidence from both their experiences and from their research to write hypotheses.
facts and details—facts are things that are known to be true; they often answer the questions *who*, *what*, *where*, *when*, *why*, or *how*. Details are examples that expand on an idea, including descriptions, quotes, analyses, statistics, anecdotes, or reasons.	Maurice has to write a report on the world's most dangerous volcano. He does research and learns that Mauna Loa in Hawaii is dangerous, but Tamu Massif, east of Japan, is bigger. After reading the facts and statistics about both volcanoes, Maurice concludes that Mauna Loa is more dangerous because Tamu Massif is completely under water. He writes a report comparing the two volcanoes and includes the facts and details he found in his research to support his conclusion.
informational/ explanatory—factual writing that demonstrates comprehension of a topic, concept, process, or procedure	Prealgebra students are asked to explain how to use factoring to solve a problem. Students solve the problem mathematically, and then write step-by-step explanations of the process they used to factor the equation. The teacher expects their explanations to include the appropriate mathematical and academic vocabulary, and they must clearly describe the order of operations.

(Continued)

Term and Definition	Example
narrative—a story, usually of a personal experience; a spoken or written account of connected events	The teacher reads a story about a dog that got lost and how it finally found its way home. After the story, the teacher asks students to write about a time they were lost. She asks them to include what happened, how they felt, and how they found their way home. Students use a story structure graphic organizer to add an introduction, description of the characters, a middle, a climax, and a resolution. The teacher provides a word bank of sequence words to help them put the events in order.
narrator—a character who recounts the events of a story or novel	Each student in the fourth-grade class is given a small plastic animal. For a week, the students take their animals everywhere, take pictures of the animal in different locations, and even collect small souvenirs from their travels. At the end of the week, each student is asked to write a narrative from the point of view of the animal. The animal is the narrator, describing the adventures it had, the places it visited, and the people it met. Students read the animal's narratives aloud to the class and display the pictures and souvenirs in scrapbooks.
opinion—a personal belief or judgment; what an individual thinks about something	Second graders are asked to select their favorite pets from a group of pictures. They work with partners and tell their classmates why they chose each pet. They are asked to use sentence frames, *In my opinion, the _____ is the best pet because _____*. After sharing their ideas, they are asked to draw pictures of their favorite pets and write their opinions.

Term and Definition	Example
sequence of events— events that come one after the other in a particular order. In a story, these may be the beginning, middle, and end; in informational writing, these may be steps in a process; in persuasive writing, the sequence may include causes and effects.	In his third-grade class, Marco is learning about settlers, including why they left their homes, how they traveled to different areas, what happened on their journey, and what life was like in their new environment. Marco works with his table group to learn about the Forty-Niners who came to California during the Gold Rush. For a final history project, Marco's group is asked to write diary entries from the perspective of a settler. Each entry represents one event in the journey. After the diary is written, the students create a storyboard sequencing the events in the order they happened.
temporal words— time-related transitions	Juno and Maribel work together with a set of pictures and a set of cards. Each card has a temporal word on it, such as *yesterday*, *meanwhile*, *after*, *before*, *once*, and *finally*. The two friends work together to order the pictures so that they tell a story. They discuss what is happening in each picture. Then, they place each word card under a corresponding picture and orally recite the story to each other, using the temporal words as sentence starters. Juno is an English learner, so she also tells the story in her heritage language and includes a translation of the temporal words.

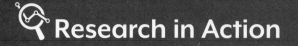

Cast Your Vote

Grades: K–1

Description

Young students are given pictures of things they could "like," along with word cards. The pictures represent objects or activities. Students choose one picture each and use words to express their opinions orally and then in writing. They include *because* to elaborate and justify their opinions.

Rationale

This strategy supports opinion/argument writing. Cast Your Vote gives young students experience with forming and justifying opinions. Students use descriptive words to explain why they like objects or activities and are introduced to a sentence structure that allows them to write their opinions and expand their thinking.

Roles and Responsibilities

Teacher: Facilitator

- Provides pictures of multiple objects and activities. Considers the students in their class and chooses pictures that will appeal to them and that are culturally relevant.

- Asks students to discuss their ideas before choosing a picture.

- Includes word cards that represent relevant adjectives, such as *fun*, *exciting*, *cute*, or *tasty*.

- Reads the words aloud, and asks students to contribute other words.

Student: Convincer

- Discusses ideas with partners or in table groups.

- Practices sentences orally before writing.

- Uses the word cards and offers additional describing words.

- Makes sure to include *because* in their responses.

Process

1. Give a set of picture cards to pairs of students. Ask students to name the objects or the activities on the cards.

2. Give students a set of word cards, including two cards that say *because*.

3. Ask each student to identify one object or one activity that they like. Have them tell their partner about the card they chose, including why they picked it. Encourage them to use the word cards in their responses.

4. Model how to create an opinion sentence and include the word *because* in a response: "I like playing soccer *because* _____." Have students practice with their partners and use the word cards as needed.

5. After students have made their choices, hold up one picture at a time and take a vote by asking how many students chose the picture. Keep a tally on the board. Ask a student who selected the picture to share their sentence explaining why they chose the picture.

6. Continue to tally votes for each picture. Once all the pictures have been voted on, model how to create a summary statement: "_____ students liked the picture of _____ because _____."

7. Have students each write a sentence about which picture they chose and why and a sentence about which picture got the most votes.

Differentiation

Write the word *because* on a different colored word card, or use a different colored marker, to call attention to this transition word. Listen in as students discuss their choices, and help them use the correct form or tense of the describing words. Create a hand signal for the word *because*. Each time a student starts to explain their reason, have them use the hand signal to remember to add the word *because* as they complete the sentence.

Closure

Grades: 2–3

Description

Students practice writing closing sentences, based on content they are learning. Closure promotes the habit of summing up their thinking by providing a final statement every time they write, in alignment with the writing standards for organization that include a concluding statement.

Rationale

Closure is satisfying. A strong closing sentence signifies more than just an ending. It reminds the reader of what they just read, provides a summary, or recalls a main idea. A closing sentence should not introduce a new idea, but it can leave the reader with something to think about or ponder. Practicing closing sentences across content areas reinforces the importance of this writing component, which is why this strategy is effective across multiple writing genres. In informational writing, the closing sentence can signify the final step in a process; in persuasive writing, the closing statement can finalize an argument; and in a narrative, the concluding statement is often the "happily ever after" moment that readers expect.

Roles and Responsibilities

Teacher: Facilitator

- Uses mentor texts to demonstrate closing sentences.
- Provides an organizer that connects the closing to the opening.
- Introduces sentence starters and word banks.
- Asks for closing sentences across multiple writing tasks.

Student: Collector

- Collects examples of closing sentences from mentor texts.
- Includes closure in speaking and listening tasks.

Process

1. Tell students that a closing sentence, or closure, wraps up their ideas, whether they are speaking or writing. Writing should conclude with a sentence that finishes a thought, sums up the main points, or brings thinking full circle.

2. Introduce examples of closing sentences using sentence starters and word banks, such as *therefore*, *to sum up*, *finally*, or *in conclusion*.

3. Model how to use sentence starters to create closing sentences for different content areas, such as: "*Therefore*, freezing temperatures turn water into ice"; "*In conclusion*, the character was able to prove he was brave after all"; or, "*Finally*, the war ended and the soldiers were able to go home."

4. Have students work with partners to use sentence starters, words, and phrases from the word banks to write closing sentences for topics your class is studying.

5. Provide a graphic organizer that includes a place for students to create an opening idea, supporting ideas, and a closing idea. Tell students that the opening and closing are similar because they both state the main idea. The opening introduces the idea, and the closing sums up the thought.

6. Offer more examples of main ideas from different content areas, and have students fill in the opening and closing sections of the organizer. Each should reference the main idea. Show students additional word banks and sentence starters for opening paragraphs.

7. Extend thinking by reminding students that a closure should not introduce a new idea. Have them check their partners' opening and closing sentences to confirm that they are both about the same main idea.

Differentiation

During content-area instruction, ask students to orally describe what they have learned, and remind them to use closing sentences to summarize their thinking. Have students use highlighters or sticky notes to color-code opening and closing sentences in texts they are reading. Ask them to use the same color highlighter or sticky note to call out these sentences in their own writing or during peer revision. Write examples of student sentences on chart paper, and post them as additional mentor texts.

Teachers and students discover closing sentences in a variety of texts from the classroom library.

Connecting Claims

Description

Students practice writing claims and then finding evidence that supports their claims. They learn to make discriminating choices about evidence that both supports the claim and furthers the argument.

Rationale

This strategy supports opinion/argument writing as students practice finding evidence to back up their ideas. Students learn to introduce multiple sources and select the examples that best support their claims. Students learn criteria for strong evidence and how to select the best evidence to connect to their claims.

Roles and Responsibilities

Teacher: Guide

- Provides texts that offer multiple points of view or a topic that can be discussed from a cross-curricular perspective.
- Models how to refine a claim by integrating ideas from different texts.
- Thinks aloud through the revision process to show how to expand on ideas.

Student: Gatherer

- Works with partners or in small groups to discuss, read, and research.
- Collects examples of evidence that support a claim.
- Modifies claims as new information is uncovered.

Process

1. Provide a set of topics that can be discussed from different perspectives. For example, choose an event from history that had both good and bad impacts on a population; or select a controversial topic, like dress codes, that benefit some but disadvantage others.

2. Ask students to discuss their opinions about the topic in small groups or with partners. Ask them to share their different ideas and post their opinions on chart paper.

3. Ask students to help define *strong evidence* (factual, comes from an authoritative source, can be confirmed in another source). Model how to find evidence in text that supports an idea.

4. Have students write their claims above a two-column chart. Use the examples from the chart paper as inspiration. Label the left side of the chart *Evidence* and the right side *Why It Is Important*.

5. Provide text sets and internet access so that students may research the topic.

6. Model how to find evidence in the text: an exact quote, a brief summary, data, or a graphic.

7. Write or paraphrase the evidence in the left column. In the right column, demonstrate how to explain why the quote or paraphrase is important by connecting it directly to the claim. Give students sentence starters, such as *This means_____, The evidence shows_____,* or *This quote proves_____* to help them make the connection.

8. Use the checklist to determine if the phrases, data, or graphics they chose meet the criteria for strong evidence.

9. Finally, ask students to annotate their evidence, identifying if the example is meant to clarify the issue, change someone's thinking, suggest an action, or demonstrate an impact.

10. Once students have completed their organizers, have them each write a paragraph that includes the claim and the evidence they found, including how the evidence connects to the claim.

Differentiation

Start with a simple topic, and ask students to only write one paragraph, just to get comfortable with the process. Include formative assessment by monitoring as students explain their evidence to partners. Confirm that their evidence meets the established criteria before asking them to write a paragraph. Leave time for additional research so students may return to their paragraphs to further elaborate on their claims. Give explicit examples and a variety of sentence starters. (See figure 2.1 below.) Encourage students to use academic and content-specific vocabulary.

Figure 2.1—Phrases to Support Connecting Claims

Understanding the Issue	Showing Another Perspective or Changing a Way of Thinking	Clarifying the Impact of the Issue and Naming an Action
• People don't realize____, and they might____. • Knowing this will____. • Basically, this means____. • If I knew____, I would____. • The evidence shows____.	• I still believe____, but this evidence____. • This evidence changes my view____. • By focusing on____, a person might miss____. • At first glance____, but a closer look____.	• This causes____. • The effect of this is____. • If you connect these pieces of evidence, you____. • It seems clear that____. • In the end, ____.

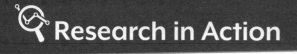

What's a Claim?

Secondary Grades

Description

Students respond to a topic with a claim that expresses how they feel. Then, they research a variety of sources, annotating the text for evidence, reasons, and counterclaims. After each source, students revisit their original claims and decide to keep them, refine them, or change them.

Rationale

In this strategy, students examine multiple sources, practice using annotation to respond to text, and use critical thinking to organize and refine their ideas. Citing and referencing the texts supports argument writing because it shows the importance of using credible sources when providing evidence.

Roles and Responsibilities

Teacher: Facilitator

- Provides protocols for students to ask questions and have discussions.
- Uses specific annotation marks to identify different responses to the reading.
- Asks students to transfer their annotations to a graphic organizer, and demonstrates the importance of citations.

Student: Investigator

- Stays engaged with the text by asking targeted questions.
- Discusses ideas orally before beginning to draft.
- Stays open to the possibility that information in the text may affect the original claim.

Process

1. Introduce a controversial topic, such as a headline from the news, a dilemma from a novel or from a historical event, or an implication of a scientific discovery. Have students do a three-minute quick-write about the topic. Tell students this is their first draft of a claim.

2. Define *claim* as their point of view or perspective about the topic.

3. Provide sheets of chart paper to small groups of students, and have them choose one student to be the recorder. Tell each group they have five minutes to list as many questions as they can think of about the topic.

4. Next, have each group place a star next to the questions that are open-ended (could have more than one answer) versus questions that are closed-ended (can be answered with *yes* or *no*). Then, have students number the questions in order of importance.

5. Point out the questions that students prioritized as the top three most important. Tell them these questions will guide their research.

6. Have students use text sets or the internet to find the answers to their top three questions. Suggest that they use annotation marks as they read, such as *A* if they found an answer to one of their questions, *E* for evidence, *R* for reasons, and *CC* for ideas that contradict their claims.

7. Provide four-square graphic organizers. Tell students to label each square, *A*, *E*, *R*, and *CC*. Have them transfer their annotations to their organizers.

8. Tell each student that now, they will revisit their original claim from their quick-write and decide if they want to keep their claim, modify it, or change it depending on what they discovered in their research.

9. Ask students to draft paragraphs that include their claims, followed by two pieces of evidence with reasons to support each piece and one counterclaim.

Differentiation

Create sentence stems that connect reasons to evidence, such as *I used to think ___, but now ___,* or *The article states ___, therefore ___.* Have students share their evidence with partners before transferring it to the graphic organizers. Ask students to make notes on their graphic organizers that reference the sources where they found their evidence. Have them include the references in their paragraphs. Ask students to reflect on the process. Have them tell partners their definition of a *claim*. **Source:** The Question Formulation Technique (QFT) was created by the Right Question Institute (RQI). Visit **rightquestion.org** for more information and free resources.

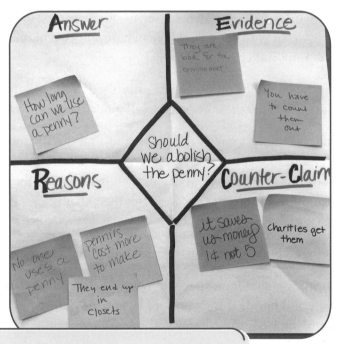

Students should have ample time to think about the pros and cons of an issue.

Moving Forward: Top Must-Dos

Explicitly teaching genre helps students recognize how the characteristics of good writing are influenced by task, audience, and purpose. Understanding the genre means the writer can make informed decisions to help readers comprehend the text. Both reading and writing in different genres helps students develop a sense of their reading and writing skills and enables them to anticipate the structure of the texts they read (Tompkins 2013).

Explicitly Teach All Writing Genres

Introduce one genre at a time, identifying the components of that genre (including when to use it), the organizational structures of the genre, the types of transitions, and the kinds of details most common to the genre. Find examples of each genre, and use these texts as mentor or model texts to analyze the writing techniques and to identify the choices made by the author. Be explicit as you think aloud during the writing process for each genre. The three most frequently encountered genres include: expository, persuasive or argumentative, and narrative writing.

Build Understanding of Genres Using Frameworks

Expository writing is explanatory or informational, like newspaper articles, reports, or even instructional materials. Expository writing can be structured as a process, a sequence, as step-by-step instructions, or as a descriptive example. Therefore, transitions are often sequential or process-oriented, such as *next*, *then*, and *finally*. Details included in expository writing tend to be specific and factual, using clear labels and precise language. Details can even take the form of diagrams or illustrations as they depict a visual explanation. Use examples from textbooks, journals, or the internet to highlight each component of the genre.

Opinion or *argumentative writing* is used to convince or persuade. Advertisements, editorials, reviews, or debates between two opposing sides are examples of persuasive writing. Argument writing starts with a claim or an opinion and then offers evidence to support or prove the claim. Persuasive writing can use a cause-and-effect structure, a problem-solution structure, or a claim-counterclaim structure. Transition words such as *if...then*, *however...*, or *therefore* reinforce these structures, and strong details such as data and statistics or emotional language appeal to the reader's rational or sentimental nature. Bring in magazine ads, and ask students how additional elements, such as images, colors, and fonts, are used to create persuasive messages. Listen to speeches, and ask students to identify the qualities of persuasive writing they can hear in the speech.

Narrative writing tells a story. It is used to recount events in a way that engages the reader. It can be fiction or nonfiction. Biographies, stories, plays, and even some poems are narratives. Narratives rely on story structures that introduce the characters, setting, and conflict, show rising action that leads to a climax, falling action, and finally, a resolution. Authors can play with structure by including flashbacks or using multiple narrators to show parallel stories in one narrative. Transition words are temporal, such as *meanwhile, at the same time, the next day,* or *later.* Details should be descriptive and reveal things about the characters or the action so the reader connects with the story and stays invested in the outcome. Point out story structures in movies, in games, in plays, and in novels. Have students identify the personal details that the author uses to make the writing come alive, and ask students to mirror that kind of authenticity in their own work.

Use Vertical Alignment to Build upon Genre Understanding

Younger students can be introduced to each genre in small steps. Ask students to describe a picture or explain something about themselves, their families, or their communities. Ask them to express an opinion and give at least one reason why they feel that way. Allow students to tell a story modeled after a story they have read. This is a great way to practice with different writing styles and encourages older elementary students to experiment with their own writing voices. Building upon this foundational understanding, middle grade students can be presented with instruction that provides more sophistication, including more components, more evidence of structure, and varied transitions and details about the range of genres. Consider using graphic novels, and show how the author used images and shapes to convey emotions, mood, and tone. Secondary students will have more experiences writing across content areas. Older students can combine more than one genre, such as writing a persuasive essay from the perspective of a virus entering a healthy body, demanding to be let in; writing poems about triangles using

> " Both reading and writing in different genres helps students develop a sense of their reading and writing skills and enables them to anticipate the structure of the texts they read (Tompkins 2013). "

metaphors and descriptive words; or writing an explanation of a historical event from the perspective of the geographical elements where the event took place. In these cases, details may align with the text type, but they will also show the student's understanding of content-specific vocabulary and concepts.

Support Genre Writing with Graphic Organizers

Use tools that help students organize their thinking. Expository writing can begin with outlines, tree maps, or Venn diagrams. These help students think about main ideas and the details that support them or can help them make comparisons and find similarities and differences. In science, provide a template for how to conduct an experiment, or use interactive notebooks with tables and charts to identify important information. In social studies, provide parallel timelines or circle maps to help place events in historical contexts.

Before starting an argument, students can create a claim, then use three-column charts to record evidence, explain what it means, and cite where it came from. By folding a sheet of paper in half, students can write one perspective on the top half of the page and an opposing perspective on the bottom half of the page. Younger students can hold up colored cards to express pros and cons about a topic. Whichever color they use the most helps them formulate their claims. These note-taking tools can be referenced during drafting and revising and may prompt rethinking of claims.

Story maps are simple organizers that help students prepare to write narratives. Use shapes like hearts or stars to represent different character traits. Encourage students to storyboard their narratives before writing. Create bar graphs to compare characters' qualities, such as *ambition*, *integrity*, or *greed*.

Engage students by making the writing process fun and creative, and show them that every stage in the process gets time and attention. Most importantly, refer to these organizers throughout the process so planning, drafting, and revising become habitual when writing.

Provide Multiple Opportunities for Each Genre

Provide opportunities for students to engage in all writing genres in multiple contexts with varying purposes. Writing does not need to always be a lengthy report or essay. Start class with a quick-write asking students to tell a story about something funny that happened to them or an accomplishment that makes them proud. During mathematics instruction, ensure that students provide written explanations of how they solved the problem, in two or three sentences, to practice using the language of math and appropriate transition words. Ask students to role play during social studies, presenting brief arguments about historical events from perspectives of different people involved.

Remember to tailor evaluation to the purpose of the assignment. If the writing was meant to show an explanation of math, then grammar or complex sentence structures may not be the most important thing to look for in the response, whereas the vocabulary and conceptual understanding should take precedence.

Further Considerations

Provide Explicit Prompts and Rubrics

Writing instruction relies on explicit writing prompts and rubrics that clearly identify what the student is expected to do. Be sure students can articulate the task, audience, and purpose of the writing. Remind them that the task is the *what*. Are they writing a letter? A report? A response? Understanding the task means understanding the format they will use. Their audience will determine tone and language choices. Will they use formal language and highly academic terms? Do they need to include specific vocabulary? The purpose represents *why* they are writing. Are they trying to convince? Entertain? Inform? Knowing the purpose influences the selection of genre, structure, and the types of details they choose to include.

Model and Release Responsibility

Allow time to model and demonstrate and release responsibility to students. Make the reading and writing connection explicit. Younger students can model their writing after mentor texts. This is a great way to introduce sentence structures and language choices, and students will feel confident and successful when they can match the style of a published writer. Older students can read text more closely to identify the text type and to make inferences about what the author was thinking based on the writing choices they made. Use annotation tools and multiple readings to help students dive deeper into the text. Revisiting texts multiple times allows students to connect more personally to the nuances of the writing, encouraging them to add these layers to their own work. Older students need to see how texts across content areas are organized. Graphics, diagrams, tabs, and icons all serve to help guide the reader through the material. Give students a tour of their textbooks before instruction. These resources are good examples of organizational options that are generalizable and can ultimately aid in comprehension. Once students know how a text works, it is easier to unpack.

Provide Time to Talk before Writing

Build in time for students to talk before they are asked to write. There are multiple strategies to promote discussion before writing. Have students brainstorm in small groups, recording their ideas on chart paper. Then, do gallery walks and have students comment on the other groups' work. Ask students to choose a side when discussing a controversial topic. Challenge them to work together to convince someone from the opposing side to join their team. Engage students in storytelling by using daily get-to-know-you questions. Remind students to use complete sentences, even when speaking casually. Encourage the use of academic language with small incentives for every time they use vocabulary words authentically. Soon, they will be looking for ways to include higher-level terms in their speech.

> Remind students to use complete sentences, even when speaking casually. Encourage the use of academic language with small incentives for every time they use vocabulary words authentically.

High Stakes State testing!
- what do tests show schools?
- Are they stressful?
- How do tests support students?
- How are tests culturally biased?
- what is the purpose?
- Are tests good for kids?
- How much time do they take?
- Are they costly?
- Do kids like them?
- How do they impact students?

> Students generate a list of questions to engage with the topic of high-stakes testing.

My Teaching Checklist

Are you ready to develop students' understanding of genre characteristics? Use this checklist to help you get started!

Genre Characteristics

Look Fors	Description
Students are given opportunities to write with a range of purposes in a variety of genres.	• Use organizers and explicit brainstorming strategies to plan writing. • Provide mentor texts for each genre. • Embed writing into daily instruction, in short and long forms.
Students are clear (through instruction and practice) about the variety of genres, and the purpose and structure of each.	• Have students annotate and highlight text they read to identify characteristics of different genres. • Post examples of different text structures along with corresponding text examples. • Ask students to identify why authors choose specific genres.
Writing is taught through the gradual release of responsibility model.	• Always model and think aloud through each stage of the writing process. • Write alongside your students so they see your process as well. • Wait to release students to independent work until you are confident they can be successful, and provide scaffolds as needed.

Chapter Summary

Writing is used to communicate ideas. The communication needs to be clear and comprehensible. A strategic way to structure writing is by being considerate of genre. Genre suggests formats and structures that will best serve the task, audience, and purpose of the writing. The three most common genres are expository, persuasive, and narrative writing. Each genre uses specific text structures, language choices, tone, and types of details that are recognizable to the reader. These characteristics help the reader make predictions and stay engaged, thus supporting comprehension. Introducing genre through mentor texts and explicitly teaching the characteristics of each genre will build students' confidence as writers. Even the youngest readers can be supported to understand genre. Giving all students multiple opportunities to write for a variety of reasons, in both short and long form, will reinforce their writing proficiency.

Reflection Questions

- How do you use mentor texts in your classroom? How can mentor texts be used to explicitly demonstrate various genres?

- How do you support writers as they work through the stages of the writing process?

- What kind of writing are students practicing across all content areas?

Chapter 3

Prewriting and Organization

Background Information and Research

When students understand how to structure writing based on genre, the process of writing can begin. At this stage, some students may think they will be hit with inspiration and just start to write. Remember, writing is a learned skill, which means students can practice and get better. The process of writing begins with prewriting and organization. Prewriting allows for the generation of ideas, and organizing is a way to put those ideas into a structure that is appropriate for the task, audience, and purpose within a genre.

Asking different writers about their prewriting strategies will likely yield a variety of answers. "While many writers have traditionally created outlines before beginning writing, there are several other effective prewriting activities. We often call these prewriting strategies 'brainstorming techniques'" (KU Writing Center 2021, para. 1). Brainstorming allows the writer the space to experiment with thoughts, to meander in various directions, until a clear writing path reveals itself. Effective brainstorming requires a safe environment where students are free to explore (and abandon) different paths and think out of the box. Keeping this stage of the process playful "can engage reluctant writers and help children learn from one another. Further, play fosters creativity and...opens up the space for inquiry and problem solving" (UNICEF 2018, 10).

There are useful strategies to support brainstorming, including list-making, developing thought clusters, and freewriting. Providing structures for brainstorming does not limit creativity. On the contrary, pushing against a structure can *foster* creativity as students try to problem-solve to meet the criteria. "In a knowledge economy where rote tasks are [or] can be completed by machines, and almost all information is available with one click, students need to be ready to learn independently, and constantly adapt, innovate, and creatively problem-solve" (Davis 2018). Brainstorming strategies can "help you with both your invention and organization of ideas and can aid you in developing topics for your writing" (KU Writing Center 2021, para. 1).

Brainstorming can be one of the first steps of the writing process. It allows for student creativity and ideas to be collated into one space. Once students have brainstormed a variety of ideas, those thoughts and ideas can be organized. "An important but often forgotten step is transitioning from a brainstorm to an organized plan. We can teach students how to organize their thinking in a way that is appropriate for the genre and will improve the quality of their written piece" (Reading Rockets 2021, para. 14). Think of a laundry basket full of socks. You might pour out the socks into a pile, and then begin sorting them, first by color, and then by style. Eventually, you may find a match for most or all of them. Similarly, students can start to connect the thoughts and ideas they generated during the brainstorm, finding creative reasons for the matches they make. Some of their thoughts might not seem to align, so these can be set aside and used later. Students can then begin to organize their ideas based on the genre of writing, the content area, or the purpose for writing. Modeling the use of graphic organizers to capture their thinking and suggesting strategies such as outlining, using tree maps, creating interactive notebooks, or using folded paper models will support students as they design their writing plans. Being creative and having fun during this process increases students' sense of agency and intrinsic motivation and encourages them to return to their notes during the drafting and revision stages for more inspiration.

> Brainstorming allows the writer the space to experiment with thoughts, to meander in various directions, until a clear writing path reveals itself. Effective brainstorming requires a safe environment where students are free to make mistakes and think out of the box.

Connection to the Rope

Scarborough's Reading Rope (2001) "illustrates the many strands that are woven into skilled reading" (Auray 2020). The strands dictate *strategy* use for increased language comprehension and practice to achieve *fluency* in word recognition. In much the same way, writing requires strategic instruction in genre, structure, and sentence-combining, as well as practice negotiating the stages of the writing process. Brainstorming ideas may produce great thinking, but students need to be guided through the process of organizing those thoughts to get ready for drafting.

To do this, students need to recognize that good writing effectively conveys meaning to the reader. "Becoming a strong writer involves learning, practicing, and coordinating all these skills. Writing may be the most difficult thing our students learn in school because it requires them to apply what they have learned as readers (phonics, vocabulary, text structure), plus additional skills (planning, considering audience, handwriting, revising, etc.) to generate their own work" (Reading Rockets 2021, para. 5).

Strategy instruction is best accomplished through guided practice with a gradual release of responsibility. For reading instruction, this means modeling strategic ways to unpack text, to examine the author's purpose and craft, and to integrate ideas from other sources to inform your understanding. For writing instruction, the teacher models the stages of the writing process, starting with brainstorming and leading to organizing. This reinforces the understanding of genre and text structure; the recognition of task, audience, and purpose in the selection of supporting details and elaboration; and the use of language such as transition words. When students begin to organize, they make decisions about these writing structures that help them shape their initial drafts. "Writing like reading is not an innate skill we are born with, it needs to be explicitly taught in order for children to learn how to do it well. When teaching direct writing instruction, the same model holds true—again reinforcing the reading/writing connection" (Auray 2020, para. 8).

Implications for Teaching and Learning

"To enable our students to write well, we need to help them by explicitly teaching the components of effective writing" (Reading Rockets 2021, para. 5). Writing is a learned skill, and as such, each step in the process deserves explicit attention. "You cannot assume that improvement will evolve without specific skill instruction or informed teacher direction" (Auray 2020, para. 11). Providing structure for brainstorming and tools to assist with organization are fundamental to help reinforce skill building and continued practice.

Gradual release in the brainstorming and organizing stage follows familiar steps. The Institute of Education Sciences Practice Guide (Graham et al. 2012) describes how to use gradual release in writing instruction, specifically for brainstorming and organizing. First, the teacher provides background knowledge, including why students should use brainstorming and how organizing their ideas will help them. For brainstorming, tell students this activity loosens their thinking and opens their creativity. For organizing, explain that tools such as charts or outlines help them visualize the structure their writing will take.

Next, the teacher describes ways to brainstorm strategically, using prompts to generate ideas. Encourage students to brainstorm in silly or unconventional ways. Stray thoughts often result in divergent thinking and creative problem-solving. Describe different ways to pull the thoughts together (like sorting the socks). Encourage students to articulate the connections they make. Are they informed by the genre? Use templates to help students make decisions about the ideas that are most relevant to the task.

Model and think aloud as you organize the thoughts from your brainstorm. Show students you are also an author, and allow them to use your sentences or sentence frames as mentor texts until they feel confident generating their own. For those who are ready, incorporate their suggestions into your writing to show that you value their contributions.

Give students time to collaborate in small groups to practice applying the techniques you have been modeling. Working with their classmates will spur new ideas and create unique connections, which will only enhance their own thinking. Plus, oral discourse is the precursor to writing. Collaboration allows students to learn and internalize academic vocabulary and complex sentence structures. Assist students as they practice using these strategies to come up with ideas, but remember to be a facilitator, asking questions of students rather than giving answers. Allowing students to have agency over their thinking will help them be more confident when they are asked to replicate the strategy independently.

Key Terms for Teacher Understanding

The following chart provides definitions of essential terms educators need to know and an example of each one.

Term and Definition	Example
brainstorming—an oral and written rehearsal of ideas in which students begin to prepare for the genre in which they will write	Kim has been given a writing assignment. She stares at the blank page and feels intimidated. She remembers that *brainstorming* means writing down as many ideas about the topic as she can think of, so she starts putting ideas on the paper. If she gets stuck, she asks herself questions, such as "What is something I wonder about this topic? Why do I like or dislike the topic? What can I learn from this topic?" She gives herself 15 minutes to brainstorm as much as she can. When time is up, she looks at her paper, now filled with words, and begins to look for patterns or connections.
clustering—a way to record thoughts and observations for a piece of writing after students have chosen a topic	Ms. Ramirez's eighth graders have just finished reading a poem by Langston Hughes, and she wants them to write three paragraphs about the poem. She models how to begin by drawing a circle in the center of a sheet of chart paper. In the circle, she writes the name of the poem. Then, in a ring around the main circle, she beings to write things she knows about the poem and about Langston Hughes. She draws circles around each of these topics and lines connecting them to the main circle in the middle. Ms. Ramirez then does the same process for the smaller circles, connecting them to the main idea and the subtopics.

(Continued)

Term and Definition	Example
diagramming—a visual organizational prewriting activity to help see relationships; writers create a concept map of how different elements fit together	The first graders in Mr. Bana's class are learning about the lifecycle of butterflies. He wants them to write a story about a caterpillar that turns into a butterfly. He gives each table a sheet of chart paper and sticky notes in different shapes and colors. Some of the sticky notes are in the shape of arrows. He explains that students should use the sticky notes to map out their stories. What happens first? What is the second thing that happens? He displays a list of transition words and reminds them to use these to show the sequence of events. Students write words or draw pictures on the sticky notes and begin placing and rearranging them on the chart paper. They write transition words on the arrow-shaped sticky notes, such as *next*, *then*, or *finally*, and place them in the appropriate places on the chart paper.
drafting—the stage of the writing process when a preliminary version of text is created	Every day for the past six weeks, Sophie's class did a five-minute quick-write before math, expressing their goals, their confusion about a problem, or explaining a strategy they used to solve the homework. Sophie now must write a reflective essay about her math journey. She rereads her entries and sees a theme of *perseverance*. She highlights places in her journal that support her theme and creates an outline to map out what she wants to write. Then, she starts to write her final paragraph first because her success is the strongest idea in her mind. After she drafts her final paragraph, she realizes the reflective essay needs to start by explaining her struggles, so she drafts that paragraph next.

Term and Definition	Example
freewriting—a prewriting strategy that involves filling a sheet of paper with ideas, without worrying about grammar, spelling, or even coherence	Jackson's science teacher shows the class a tube filled with blue liquid. He pours a yellow liquid into the tube. Jackson expected the liquid to turn green, but instead, the yellow liquid separated from the blue liquid and sank to the bottom. Jackson is asked to freewrite for seven minutes about the phenomenon in his science notebook. Using stream of consciousness, Jackson records his thoughts, questions, and ideas. He includes some drawings as well. Then, he and his tablemates share their freewrites and look for patterns. Their common questions become the basis for the start of their investigation about the phenomenon.
organizing—the arrangement of ideas, incidents, evidence, or details in a perceptible order in a paragraph, essay, or speech	Elena's ceramics teacher has asked her to write a description of her piece for the school's art show. Elena jots down several ideas, including what inspired her, the process she used to create it, how she feels about the piece, and what it represents. She knows she only has a half-page in the program, so she structures her ideas from most important to least important. She starts with what it represents, then describes her inspiration, and how she feels about it. Finally, she explains how she made it.

(Continued)

Term and Definition	Example
outlining—a plan for the paper that will help writers organize and structure their ideas in a way that effectively communicates the ideas to readers and supports the thesis statement	Jenna is ready to write her college essay. She has generated a list of her accomplishments, some of the challenges she has overcome, and several reasons why she chose this college. Before she begins drafting, she decides to use an outline to organize her thoughts. She lists the first topic, *Why I chose this college*, and then uses bullets to list three main reasons: it supports the local community, it has great research facilities, and it is committed to social justice. The next topic is her *Accomplishments*. She lists two bullets: winning class vice president and raising money for a local charity. Finally, she writes *Challenges* and lists two major challenges she overcame in her life: moving to a new town and being cut from the track team. As she rereads her outline, she is able to see a pattern—she has always faced life with optimism. She decides to use the theme of *optimism* in her thesis statement.
prewriting—the stage of the writing process when writers develop goals, generate ideas, gather information, organize ideas, and develop a logical structure	Jamal has been doing research on Spain for a report. He has gathered lots of information on note cards, but he is not sure where to start. He begins to sort the cards into categories: History, Art and Literature, and Climate and Geography. He has a few cards that do not seem to fit anywhere, so he sets those aside for later. After looking over his notes, he thinks about which category to write about first. It seems most logical to go from general to specific, so he starts with Climate and Geography, followed by History, and then Art and Literature. He begins organizing the cards within each category to form the foundation of his draft.

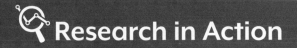

Blueprint

Grades: K–1

Description

This visualizing strategy is a way for teachers to guide the brainstorming process. The teacher asks a series of questions that help students picture a scene before drawing pictures or writing stories. Students use sensory details to label their drawings or to enhance their stories.

Rationale

Descriptive writing includes details that paint a picture for the reader. Younger students can start to practice writing descriptions with sensory and emotional words, using simple but complete sentences and including some punctuation. Guided imagery helps them focus on the sights, sounds, colors, and feelings they want to express.

Roles and Responsibilities

Teacher: Input-Provider

- Asks students to brainstorm sensory words and posts them for their reference.
- Provides pictures for inspiration before beginning a visualization exercise.
- Uses a graphic organizer with symbols representing each of the five senses. Models how to use this tool to record details.

Student: Visualizer or Describer

- Practices describing orally before writing.
- Uses word cards with pictures to describe feelings.

Process

1. Tell students they are about to do a visualizing exercise as a way to brainstorm before they begin drafting. Explain that *visualizing* means seeing something in your mind and imagining what it looks like, sounds like, feels like, and so on. Let them know that visualizing is a way to help them be descriptive in their writing.

2. Give students a graphic organizer that identifies the five senses: sight, sound, touch, taste, and smell. (See page 79 for an example.) Ask them to share examples about each of the senses, such as *Smells can be sweet*, or *Sounds can be loud*. Chart any words they may want to use later.

3. Ask students to close their eyes. Tell them to each imagine a place that is special to them. It could be their home, a relative's home, a park, or some other place that they enjoy. They do not need to share at this time. They are simply picturing the places in their minds.

4. Ask students to look around the places they are imagining. What colors do they see? What are some objects around them? Have them think of the names of the objects. Are they cold or warm?

5. Ask students if anyone is there with them in their visualizations. Who is it? What are they doing? What are they wearing? Are they close by or far away?

6. Tell students to breathe in deeply while they are imagining the locations. Do they smell anything? What does it smell like? Use example words, such as *sweet*, *salty*, or *burning*.

7. Ask students what they hear in the locations. Are there loud or soft sounds? Is there anything they can touch there? What does it feel like? Use example words, such as *soft*, *scratchy*, or *rough*.

8. After students have spent a few minutes visualizing, have them open their eyes and tell partners about their locations. Remind partners to ask questions about the sensory things they saw, felt, heard, and touched.

9. Tell students that they will each draw a picture of their location and label it or write sentences about it. To get them started, they can enter their description words on the graphic organizer first as a prewriting activity.

10. Ask a few students to share their locations. Post the pictures and descriptions around the room, and remind students that they can always visit this happy place in their minds.

Differentiation

Allow students to use emojis to help them express different feelings. They can create some of their own emojis as well. Use icons to remind students about the five senses, and provide word banks of sensory words. Ask students to draw pictures of different sensory or feeling words, and ask multilingual students to add words from their heritage languages. Encourage students to use different words from their partners. Demonstrate how being more specific improves their descriptions. Students can also practice this activity as an I Spy game with partners, describing a place or object until their partners guess what they are describing.

Looks like . . .	
Sounds like . . .	
Feels like . . .	
Smells like . . .	
Tastes like . . .	

Group Idea Mapping

Grades: 2–3

Description

In this brainstorming activity, students work together in small groups to sort ideas and to make visual connections between ideas, using sticky notes, drawings, or online applications. Students must collaborate to find connections.

Rationale

Mapping is a way to capture and organize the ideas of a group on any topic and to represent those ideas visually. Because of the diversity of the group, this exercise stimulates creative connections and provides an opportunity for analytical problem-solving as the group works to form connections between varied concepts.

Roles and Responsibilities

Teacher: Facilitator

- Models multiple ways to represent ideas visually.
- Allows sentence fragments or drawings for this activity.
- Introduces guiding questions to assist if students get stuck.
- Gives students roles, such as recorder, presenter, or facilitator, to ensure participation from all.

Student: Contributor

- Generates as many ideas as possible.
- Understands that all ideas are accepted.
- Has permission to ask clarifying questions.
- Looks for and honors connections that may not be obvious.

Process

1. Have students work in small groups. Distribute a sheet of chart paper to each group, and ask them to write the name of the topic in the center of the paper.

2. Tell students they each must contribute ideas about the topic. Have them take turns. The first student adds an idea and draws a line connecting it to the topic. The next student can either add a new idea or add a connection to the first student's idea, and so on. Each student must explain their connection.

3. After each student has been able to contribute at least three ideas, ask them to discuss what they notice about the connections they made.

4. Ask students to do a gallery walk and visit each of the other maps. Tell them to return to their own maps and each add one more connection if needed, based on the ideas they observed from the other groups.

5. Ask the groups to identify the strongest connections and to be ready to explain their thinking. Have a member of each group share about the connections they made and explain the connections.

6. Tell students they are now ready to begin organizing their own writing, using the chart paper to guide their thinking. Have them use an outline or another writing template to start planning their drafts.

Differentiation

Give students a time limit to generate ideas to spur thinking. Have students use different-colored sticky notes or markers to represent different categories of ideas. Add linking words to the connecting lines, such as *because, similar to*, or *results in*, to guide students as they transition to drafting. If using an online application, have students choose unique fonts or colors to represent their own ideas or to organize ideas. As a variation, use subtopics of a bigger idea for each group's map. During the gallery walk, ask students to prioritize three of the subtopics they would choose to include in a writing assignment about the larger topic.

Looping

Grades: 4–5

Description

In Looping, students start to freewrite about a topic. Then, they choose one key thought or idea as the starting point for a new freewrite. The process continues in this way for several more rounds, with each subsequent freewrite becoming more and more specific, until a clear topic reveals itself.

Rationale

Looping is a brainstorming technique that allows students to continually refocus ideas to help them discover a writing topic or thesis. This process fosters creativity through discovery and shows students they can refocus and go in a new direction if they get stuck during their brainstorming. Looping also minimizes a student's self-criticism, as they are given permission to dive into any aspect of a topic and see where it takes them.

Roles and Responsibilities

Teacher: Director

- Prepares a set of general topics to start the process.
- Gives time limits for each "loop" to enhance urgency and foster creative thinking.
- Provides sentence starters or guiding questions to assist students as needed.

Student: Player

- Chooses the direction of each subsequent freewrite.
- Writes continually during each "loop" until the time is up.
- Identifies common themes or recurring ideas.

Process

1. Distribute a topic card and several sheets of paper to each student. Have them keep the card facedown until told to turn it over.

2. Explain to students that they will be given a set amount of time (about 5 to 10 minutes) to freewrite as much as they can about the topic on their cards. They should write without stopping and not worry about using complete sentences or proper grammar. Have students turn over their cards. Tell them to write the topic in the middle of the pages and circle it. Then, set the timer and have them start to freewrite.

3. When the time is up, tell students to put down their pencils. Ask them to read over what they wrote and identify one key idea. This could be something recurring in their freewrites or an idea that they would like to investigate a little further. Or it could be something they wrote that surprised them. Have each student circle the word or idea and then write it in the center of a new sheet of paper. Set the timer again, and tell students to freewrite about these new topics.

4. Repeat this process for at least three rounds. When the final time is up, ask students to study their freewrites and to discuss the progression of their ideas with partners. Have them explain the connections they made and the relationships to the first topics they wrote about.

5. Have students each write a thesis statement based on the progression of ideas from their various "loops."

Differentiation

Give students half-sheets of paper instead of full sheets, since a full sheet can be overwhelming and students may feel more comfortable knowing they do not have to fill up so much blank space. Monitor students as they explain their connections to their partners, and provide sentence starters and word banks to assist them with linking words. If students have trouble, encourage them to draw or doodle instead, or provide guiding questions to get them started. If using an online application, have students copy and paste the main idea from each loop onto a new blank page.

Power Notes

Secondary Grades

Description

Power Notes is a strategy for students to use to respond to or summarize material they have read. Students assign numbers to their main ideas and details to visually display the differences between main ideas and details in an outline form. Main ideas are Power 1 ideas, and details or examples are either Power 2, 3, or 4 ideas.

Rationale

Power Notes help students organize their ideas from most to least important as they create an outline before they begin to draft. Assigning numbers gives an easy visual way to sort information and to remember to include every detail that supports each main idea.

Roles and Responsibilities

Teacher: Planner

- Thinks aloud to demonstrate how to select and number the main ideas and details.

- Encourages use of graphic organizers or templates.

- Asks students to include citation information as they take notes.

- Follows up with revision activities that refer to the Power Notes.

Student: Researcher

- Annotates the text to find information quickly when needed.

- Discusses ideas orally before assigning numeric values.

- Uses content-specific and academic vocabulary as well as appropriate transition words.

Process

1. Introduce a graphic organizer, such as a tree map or an outline template, with a space to write a topic and spaces to add two or three main ideas and two or three supporting details for each idea.

2. Model how to read and annotate text to select several examples of information that explain the topic. Ask students to discuss with partners which of the evidence could be a main idea and which represents a supporting detail.

3. Ask students to label the main idea as *Power Idea 1* in their graphic organizers. Have them work together to number the details in order of significance or importance as *Power Ideas 2, 3*, and *4*. Have them record the details in their graphic organizers.

4. Monitor students as they discuss, and ask several students to share justifications for their decisions. Give them time to re-evaluate their selections and make changes as needed.

5. Have partners continue to work together to annotate a new piece of text and to record a new main idea and supporting details in the same manner. Listen as the partners discuss how they decided to number the main ideas and details.

6. Ask students to work independently to annotate a third piece of text and to number the main idea *Power Idea 1* and the supporting details as *Power Ideas 2, 3*, and *4*.

7. Tell students to use the graphic organizer as a basis for an outline, and ask them to each begin writing a draft about the topic, using the three main ideas labeled as *Power Idea 1* to create a thesis statement.

8. Remind students that each Power Idea 1 becomes the topic sentence of a supporting paragraph, and the Power Ideas 2, 3, and 4 become the details used to explain and justify the main ideas.

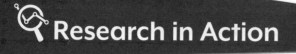

Differentiation

In **language arts**, show how to distinguish using exact quotes versus paraphrasing or summarizing, and demonstrate citation techniques for each example. In **mathematics**, ask students to generalize the steps used to solve a problem as Power Idea 1 and to use an alternative problem-solving strategy as the next Power Idea 1 to serve as a way to prove their solutions are correct. In **science**, have students provide different possible explanations for a phenomenon as their Power Idea 1, with specific examples or justifications as Power Ideas 2, 3, and 4. In **social studies**, ask students to address geographic context, economic context, or legislative context as each Power Idea 1, and to use multiple sources of information to represent different perspectives as each Power Idea 2, 3, and 4.

Moving Forward: Top Must-Dos

It is important that students engage in prewriting activities, such as brainstorming, before they begin to organize and plan their writing. Part of the brainstorming process should include opportunities to discuss their ideas with their peers as "oral and written rehearsal of ideas in which students begin to prepare for the genre in which they will write" (Reading Rockets 2021, para. 6). Social interactions keep the process fun, which fosters creativity. More importantly, brainstorming allows students to try out ideas in a safe way, without concern for being graded or critiqued. When students have a good number of ideas to work with, they can organize them, thereby making choices about how to plan their drafts. Give them tools such as graphic organizers to help with this step, and model how to use them. "Students need systematic instruction and lots of practice to understand what it takes to produce good writing. Intentional exercises, in all stages of the writing process, can help all writers to become better and struggling writers to find success" (Reading Rockets 2021, para. 40).

Extend the Brainstorming

Allow brainstorming to go beyond just the topic. Use strategies like Looping to show students how to find connections that may not have been immediately apparent. Challenge them to go further and dig deeper by using concept maps to explore different perspectives and subtopics. Let students ask questions that take them in different directions from where they thought they were going. Gamify the activities to promote rapid and unfettered thinking. From these experiences, students will feel comfortable being more expressive. And be sure students have chances to talk about their ideas before they begin to plan their writing.

Revisit Prewriting

Remember, the writing process is recursive. That means there is no specific order to it. Suppose the brainstorming exercise leads students toward a different topic. Tell them they may go back and revise their prewriting. They may notice, for example, that while they are outlining, they have more or less information about a topic than they thought. It is okay to reorganize. Revisiting the brainstorming with colored markers or sticky notes will help students see their recurring thoughts, which will most likely make for a stronger piece of writing. Have students try out different versions of their prewriting with partners, and give them guiding questions to ask each other to support the possibility of revising at this stage.

Use Structure to Students' Advantage

Sometimes, too much freedom can be overwhelming, especially for students who are not confident writers. They may feel intimidated by a blank page or freeze up when asked to "think of anything" during a brainstorm. These students can benefit from a more structured activity. In this case, use the five *W* and *H* questions: *Who? What? Where? When? Why? How?* "The journalists' questions are a powerful way to develop a great deal of information about a topic very quickly" (KU Writing Center 2021, para. 13). This scaffold can be gradually removed as students become more comfortable exploring a topic and generating questions on their own.

Further Considerations

Random Brainstorming Is Not Enough

Preface the brainstorming with intentional activities designed to spark students' interest and imagination. For example, introduce vocabulary that students will need to include in their writing. Have them include the words in their brainstorming and prewriting work so they realize the importance of using the correct terminology. Even during brainstorming, encourage students to use the appropriate linking words so they are already thinking of ways to create complex sentences. Honor every contribution, even if it does not seem relevant at the time. Save it on a sticky note, and see if it can be used later. Encourage students to think metacognitively while they plan and organize. They can ask themselves, "Did I get as much information as I needed to support this idea? Do I need to add more details? Is this main idea really the most important thing about the topic?" Stop and model using think-alouds to give students permission to pause, slow down, and reconsider through every stage of the writing process.

My Teaching Checklist

Are you ready to engage students in prewriting and organizing activities before they begin writing? Use this checklist to help you get started!

Prewriting and Organization

Look Fors	Description
Students experience explicit and systematic instruction in prewriting and organizing.	• Use explicit brainstorming strategies. • Model different ways to record thinking and plan for drafting.
Instruction is scaffolded as needed, and enough practice is provided so responsibility can gradually be released to students.	• Break processes down into simple steps, and only practice one step at a time. • Avoid moving on until students can demonstrate mastery. • Listen in on partner and small group work to check that student thinking is visible.
Graphic organizers are provided.	• Remind students that these are tools to help them produce a piece of writing; successful completion of the organizer is not the goal of the activity. • Use different types of organizers and tools, including maps, color-coding, folded papers, and more, and ask students to notice which tools they like best so they can self-select in the future.

Chapter Summary

Getting ready to write should be a relaxed and fun experience. Writing can trigger vulnerability in students, so giving them comfortable ways to get ready will lower their anxiety and foster more creative thinking. Provide a combination of free-style brainstorming strategies with more directive organizing techniques, and place less importance on spelling or grammar or even random thoughts that do not seem to relate. It is more important for students to have a flow of ideas, which they will have when they feel comfortable and accepted. Remind students that this process is valuable not only for writing but any time they are faced with a challenging assignment. Taking a few moments to think about the assignment, even in nontraditional ways, will open their minds to new possibilities. Tell students that most authors spend lots of time brainstorming and planning before they ever sit down to write, and the planning is usually evident in the quality of the final outcome.

Reflection Questions

- How do you create a welcoming environment where students feel safe to take academic risks through brainstorming?

- What kind of discussion opportunities do your students have before they try to write?

- What are challenges you foresee in these brainstorming activities? What could you do to overcome them?

Chapter 4

Revise for Purpose: Syntax of Sentences and Beyond

From the Classroom

It is imperative that students of all ages gain the skills to revise and edit their own writing. I've found this process takes time and practice. The revision process takes longer than the drafting process. It is always difficult for students to find their own writing errors. They figure that if they worked on it (especially if they typed it), then it must be good. I teach revising and editing in steps, breaking it down. A useful idea for students is "A Good Writer CARES" (Fleisher, Fout, and Ready 2003, 13). Each letter in CARES stands for a revision step:

> **C**hange a word
>
> **A**dd details, ideas, dialogue, figurative language
>
> **R**earrange the order of words, sentences, paragraphs
>
> **E**liminate wordiness or off-topic details
>
> **S**tandardize spelling, grammar, and punctuation

I spend at least a couple of days on each step. At first, we go low-tech, using print copies of everything until students are proficient. I might provide an excerpt of a "Justin" chapter from R. J. Palacio's *Wonder*, or work that the students have previously written. We use fun colors—one for each step—and double-spacing in printed copies of student work. I tell students, "Don't be afraid to annotate." They have the opportunity to talk to each other, not just mark up someone else's draft. They read the drafts aloud and hear the words. Pairs work well.

Pro Tip: Use age-appropriate print dictionaries, thesauruses, and word lists. What's more engaging than books? Use this technique with any age. There are many ways to change up revising and editing instruction. Have fun; happy revising!

—Amy Piecuch
Former Middle School Teacher
Fox River Grove Middle School
Fox River Grove, Illinois

Background Information and Research

When learning to play a sport, the coach will start the first practice with a set of drills. To the player, this may not seem to relate to the game at all. But the coach knows that the player must develop muscle memory first and learn the discrete movements involved in each aspect of the sport, e.g., the proper stance for batting, the correct hand and wrist position for shooting a basket, or the specific posture required to accurately swing a golf club. The coach will have the players make small adjustments and practice repeatedly until the optimum result is achieved— they hit the ball, make the basket, or brush the tee. Once the player can master the discrete skills, the coach can have them put it all together in the context of a game, and the player can learn when to use different skill sets for different purposes. Similarly, in playing a keyboard, the student first learns scales. Memorizing the relationship between the notes and the finger positions is foundational before the student can even think of playing music. The teacher has the student make small adjustments and practice repeatedly so they can reach the keys or switch chords quickly. Music is achieved by putting the notes together, understanding that different combinations result in different styles, tempos, and rhythms. In much the same way, learning to be a proficient writer means understanding the component parts and then practicing those multiple times. A writer may need to make adjustments at the sentence or even the word level. Then, they can start to combine words and sentences into paragraphs. Eventually, the writer will be able to put those parts together in interesting ways, appropriate to the task or the purpose of the writing. In writing, the component parts are words and sentences, and the arrangement of these parts is *syntax*.

Good writing is not just the result of extensive reading. Reading is important because it shows students writing from the reader's perspective. Students can analyze the choices made by the author. "[A]nalysis must be explicitly taught as an integral step in both reading and writing instruction. In understanding these concepts, they begin to read with 'author's eyes'" (Auray 2020, para. 13). But identifying the author's choices is not enough to make the student a good writer. "The assumption has been that if students read enough, they'll simply pick up writing skills through a kind of osmosis. But writing is the hardest thing we ask students to do, and the evidence is clear that very few students become good writers on their own" (Hochman and Wexler 2017, para. 31).

Taking the cue from sports and music, students need to practice writing at the word and word-combining levels. They use feedback from teachers and peers to make small adjustments to their sentences until they have a bank of complex sentence structures easily accessible in their minds. "Powerful writing is informed by numerous discrete skills that, when practiced over time, will inform and empower the resulting writing" (Auray 2020, para. 12). For writers, the discrete skills include parts of speech, grammar, punctuation, and connectives (words that join sentence fragments together). Without explicit instruction, students will be stuck writing simple sentences consisting of subject-verb combinations. Students certainly have more to say than this, they just need the key to unlock the ideas. That key is syntax.

> " Powerful writing is informed by numerous discrete skills that, when practiced over time, will inform and empower the resulting writing.
> —Dea Auray (2020, para. 12) "

"English parts of speech often follow ordering patterns in sentences and clauses, such as compound sentences are joined by conjunctions (*and*, *but*, *or*) or that multiple adjectives modifying the same noun follow a particular order according to their class....The rules of how to order words help the language parts make sense" (Nordquist 2020, para. 5).

Connection to the Ropes

In looking at the Reading Rope, the language comprehension strands require building background knowledge, mastering vocabulary, and showcasing language structures. Joan Sedita's "The Strands That Are Woven into Skilled Writing" (2019) explains that critical thinking skills such as generating ideas, organizing, drafting, and revising—the steps of the writing process—are best taught when students are "metacognitive and purposeful about working recursively through the stages of the writing process, and they benefit from explicit instruction in revising and editing strategies." Metacognition helps students be strategic: "Eventually, as students become more experienced writers, they will use these strategies automatically to write effectively" (Graham et al. 2016, 7). For example, using graphic organizers, mnemonic devices, or planning tools are strategies that students can turn to when they need to brainstorm, set writing goals, or outline. But the more automatic skills involved in writing—like use of grammar, punctuation, and spelling—require fluency that is achieved by repeated practice and targeted feedback. Traditionally, these skills were taught out of context, as stand-alone activities. Many of us are familiar with weekly spelling tests and worksheets that asked us to identify the direct object in a sentence. Research is showing that these skills need to be woven into authentic writing tasks and, ideally, within content-area instruction. In a 2017 essay in *American Educator*, Hochman and Wexler addressed the need for explicit writing instruction that was taught contextually, within content areas. This idea bucked tradition, which the authors explained had dictated that they teach skills in isolation. They noted, "We stopped teaching the mechanics of writing in isolation as a set of rules and definitions. Instead, we asked students at all grade levels to write about the content they were learning and then used their writing to give specific guidance." Specific guidance refers to feedback such as, "'Use an appositive in your topic sentence,' 'Put your strongest argument last,' 'Use transitions when presenting your points,' or 'Try starting your thesis statement with a subordinating conjunction'" (2017, 32).

> Students often believe they should write just like they speak, but they do not realize that writing serves a different communication purpose than speaking.

Students often believe they should write just like they speak, but they do not realize that writing serves a different communication purpose than speaking. "Precision in word choice is less exacting in informal contexts than formal ones, and grammar rules are more flexible in spoken language than in formal written language" (Nordquist 2020, para. 11). Good writing "involves more complex sentence structures and a more varied and precise vocabulary than spoken language" (Hochman and Wexler 2017, 34).

Furthermore, students should write about the content they are studying. "Many students have written nothing except narratives in elementary and middle school, often about their personal experiences. That kind of writing doesn't prepare them for the demands of high school, college, or the workforce…. [T]o maximize the benefits of writing instruction, students should start practicing their writing skills on topics embedded in content as soon as possible" (Hochman and Wexler 2017, 31, 35).

Implications for Teaching and Learning

"Structured opportunities to practice composition include building sentences, learning syntax, and forming paragraphs" (Auray 2020, para. 14). Students should grow as writers to include sentences that are varied in length and construction. These will be more engaging to their readers and will encourage them to find more interesting ways to convey meaning. Explicitly teaching sentence-level skills is imperative so students begin to practice creating more interesting sentences. These skills include "using subordinating conjunctions, appositives, and other techniques to vary their sentence structure and inserting transition words and phrases between sentences and paragraphs to make them flow" (Hochman and Wexler 2017, 37).

Explicit instruction in this foundational writing piece follows a modified version of the Gradual Release model, called the Model-Practice-Reflect instructional cycle. "Students observe a strategy in use, practice the strategy on their own, and evaluate their writing and use of the strategy" (Graham et al. 2016, 6). For example, a teacher models how to combine two simple sentences using a conjunction to create a compound or complex sentence. Students then practice by using conjunctions to combine simple sentences that they find in their own writing or in the writing of peers. They revisit the writing with the new sentences and reflect on the effect of the change on the piece. Did the new sentence make the meaning clearer? Did it make the writing easier to comprehend? Or was it simply more interesting to read? "By learning from teachers, peer models, and their own written work, students can internalize the features of effective writing and develop effective writing strategies, skills, and knowledge. Writing practice without

> " A writer who can't compose a decent sentence will never produce a decent essay—or even a decent paragraph.
>
> —Judith Hochman and Natalie Wexler (2017, para. 34) "

reflection does not provide students with opportunities to internalize important features of writing or think about how to apply learned skills and strategies effectively in new situations" (Graham et al. 2016, 19).

"Teachers should focus sentence-level instruction on sentence construction, encouraging students to consider the meaning and syntax of the sentences they develop. Teachers also should explicitly demonstrate how sentence construction and sentence mechanics, such as punctuation and capitalization, interact to form strong sentences" (Graham et al. 2012, 30). Start with the concept of a *sentence*: conveying an idea with a noun and a verb, using punctuation and proper spelling for clarity. Then, use students' own writing to revise using more complex conventions. Base the writing in content-area instruction, which will embed reading comprehension skills. For example, model how to use appositives by annotating content-area text, underlining appositives in sentences. Then, ask students to respond to text, and provide sentence starters that require the addition of an appositive: *George Washington, _____, is often called the father of our country.* Students will have to do some critical thinking to pull the appropriate information from the text that meets the criteria of the sentence construction.

Some other considerations for writing instruction include "modeling statement examples with identified errors and corrections" (Graham et al. 2016, 19) and using "rubrics to prompt students to identify ways in which their writing could be improved, and ask students to identify strengths in their writing and others' writing" (26).

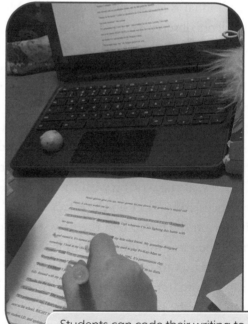

"A writer who can't compose a decent sentence will never produce a decent essay—or even a decent paragraph" (Hochman and Wexler 2017, 34). Start with the discrete skills that will give students the muscle memory to be writing champions.

Students can code their writing to make editing and revision concrete and visual.

Key Terms for Teacher Understanding

The following chart provides definitions of essential terms educators need to know and an example of each one.

Term and Definition	Example
clause—a word grouping that contains a subject and a verb; *independent clauses* convey complete meanings and can stand alone as simple sentences; *dependent clauses* do not express complete ideas on their own and must be paired with another clause	Ms. Huang gives a mini-lesson on punctuation during writing time to teach students how to join independent and dependent clauses. She asks each student to peer edit a partner's draft, looking for examples of independent clauses and dependent clauses. After students have highlighted each of these, drafts are returned to their owners. Students are then taught how to use a comma to attach a dependent clause before the independent clause; if they attach it at the end of the independent clause, no comma is needed. Students edit the sentences that were highlighted.
cohesion—cohesion is when the prose is clear and easy to understand, with all ideas presented in an orderly manner and tied together in a logical way; the use of explicit techniques to indicate the relationships among different parts of the text	Connor is assigned an argumentative essay about the historical era that promoted Manifest Destiny. After Connor finishes his draft, his teacher gives him some feedback to revise for cohesion. Connor revisits his draft and looks for ways to make the structure more logical by explaining events in sequential order. Then, he replaces some of the passive verbs with active verbs, because the essay is about movement. Finally, he uses words and phrases that have more positive connotations to support his claim and uses words with more negative connotations to describe the counterclaims to influence and convince the reader.

(Continued)

Term and Definition	Example
complex sentence—a sentence with at least one independent clause and one dependent clause	Maya's social studies essay is about the Founding Fathers. She looks at the list of facts she has compiled. As she begins drafting her essay, she adds dependent clauses with words such as *who* or *which* to provide more information about each person or event. Sometimes, she uses words such as *if* or *unless* to add a condition statement.
compound sentence—a sentence with at least two independent clauses and no dependent clauses; the independent clauses can be linked by a comma, semicolon, dash, or conjunction	Alejandro adds notes to his science notebook. When Alejandro's notebook is returned to him, the comments suggest that he make the writing flow. He asks his teacher how to do that. She suggests using compound sentences to make the paragraph less choppy. Alejandro returns to his notebook and begins finding ways to combine sentences. He realizes he needs to use punctuation in some cases and conjunctions in other cases.
compound-complex sentence—a sentence with at least two independent clauses and at least one dependent clause	In Advanced Composition, students examine the writing styles of famous authors and dissect the sentence structures they use. They identify this sentence from Jane Austen's *Pride and Prejudice* as a compound-complex sentence: "It is a truth universally acknowledged that a single man in possession of a good fortune, must be in want of a wife."

Term and Definition	Example
conjunction—a word that joins two grammatical elements of the same sentence or construction; words that illustrate the meaning between two clauses, such as *and*, *but*, or *or*	Clara is in first grade. Today, she is learning to use conjunctions to combine two ideas in one sentence. Her set of sentences reads, "Does Janie have a seed? Is it a stone? Janie plants the seed. Janie covers the seed with dirt. The sun is hot. Janie gives the seed water. The seed starts to grow." Clara uses conjunctions to write, "Does Janie have a seed *or* a stone? Janie plants the seed *and* covers the seed with dirt. The sun is hot, *but* Janie gives the seed water. The seed starts to grow."
direct object—the thing that is being acted upon by the subject; it receives the action of the verb	Writing an explanation about how to solve a math problem is a practical way to emphasize direct objects. Rafael knows that the action verbs he will use include *add*, *subtract*, *multiply*, *carry*, or *bring down*. The direct object must be the numeral that is receiving the action of the verb.
expanding sentences—the process of adding more words, phrases, or clauses	Mr. Thet notices that students have overused simple sentences in their drafts. He addresses this in a mini-lesson using student examples. He writes several simple sentences on the board: *The doorbell rang. My father answered the door. The dog was surprised.* Then, Mr. Thet creates word banks. One word bank contains adverbs and adjectives. He tells the students to add at least one adverb and one adjective to each simple sentence. The next word bank contains adverb and adjective clauses, such as *louder than expected* or *more quickly than before*. Students then add an adverbial clause to each sentence. The third word bank contains appositives, such as *a slow man* or *a small terrier*. Students add appositives to the sentences. Finally, students revise their drafts expanding at least three sentences in one of the ways they just learned.

(Continued)

Term and Definition	Example
mentor text—a piece of writing that serves as a model or an illustrative example that teachers and students read and reread for different purposes; any format of writing can serve as a mentor text: poem, argumentative essay, introduction, transition sentences	In order to help her students learn to write like scientists, biology teacher Ms. Adams uses actual research reports from medical journals as mentor texts. Together, they identify the text structure and use annotation and highlighting to call out the specific components and characteristics of scientific writing. She has her students practice one component at a time with guided practice and then looks for the use of each component in the students' final drafts.
phrase—a group of two or more words functioning as a meaningful unit within a sentence or clause; a phrase does not contain a subject-verb pairing	Jabari's seventh-grade class has been studying poetry. The teacher has been explaining how poets use phrases. As practice, Jabari's class learns about five types of phrases: noun phrases, verb phrases, adjective phrases, adverb phrases, and prepositional phrases. Jabari works with his table group to write one of each kind of phrase about a set of photos and illustrations the teacher provided. Then, the group is asked to choose one of the pictures, create a poem about it, and include one of each type of phrase in their poem.
predicate—the part of the sentence that usually contains a verb and describes the subject or shows action	After students have highlighted the subjects of each sentence, Mr. Reynolds asks them to underline the predicate, which starts with the verb that shows the action of the sentence or that describes the subject. Mr. Reynolds collects the papers and mixes up the subjects and predicates for a practice activity the next day, asking students to connect subjects and predicates in a logical way.

Term and Definition	Example
revision—the stage of the writing process when the author reviews, alters, and amends the content of writing by adding, deleting, or rearranging to clarify or enhance meaning	Ms. Morales asked students to write summaries of the photosynthesis unit. Tanya has gone through her notes and created a draft that explains the experiment they conducted in class and includes notes she pulled from her textbook. She sets it aside for a day and then rereads what she has written. She notices that some of the research from the text could be inserted into her description of the experiment to help explain the process steps and the outcomes. She makes notations in her draft about where she wants to insert the research and then begins to cut-and-paste on her computer.
simple sentence—contains a subject and a verb and expresses a complete thought; it might contain other components as well but only requires a subject and verb to be a simple sentence	Ryan's kindergarten teacher gives each student several pictures, such as a dog, a bird, a baby, a bee, and a kite. Ryan looks at each picture and tells his partner what each thing can do, such as: *a dog can bark or run or dig*; *a bird can fly or sing*. After sharing, the students are each given a sheet of paper to write simple sentences that contain the name of the item in the picture (this is the subject of the sentence) and what that thing is doing (this is the verb). Ryan writes several simple sentences and then draws a picture of a dog and a kite.
subject—the person, place, or thing that is performing the action of the sentence; the subject represents what or whom the sentence is about	Mr. Lents asks his fifth-grade students to work with partners and exchange their narrative drafts. He tells them to read the drafts and to highlight the subject of each sentence, which they can find by determining *who* or *what* is doing the action, or *who* or *what* is being described. He reminds students that looking for nouns and proper nouns can help identify the subject and warns them to not be confused by prepositional phrases, which may contain a noun.

(Continued)

Term and Definition	Example
syntactic awareness—the ability to monitor the relationships among the words in a sentence to understand while reading or composing orally or in writing	Javier and Samira are practicing a presentation. Samira stops at one of their slides and says that something doesn't sound right. They revisit the slide and reread their notes silently, then they read them aloud. Samira realizes they used a plural form of the verb, but the subject of their sentence is singular. While Samira does not specifically cite verb conjugation, she explains to Javier that they need to revise the sentence so that the subject and the verb "agree." She uses the correct verb to show him how it sounds, and he understands and revises the slide. Then, the two of them check the remaining slides, editing for verb agreement.
syntax—the order in which words are arranged in a spoken or written sentence; the arrangement of words and phrases to create well-formed sentences	Curtis is writing an informational paragraph about the rainforest. As he is revising his draft, he notices one sentence that his teacher circled. She said to check the syntax. The sentence reads, "The trees are being cleared sadly for farmland." The placement of *sadly* after the verb phrase *being cleared* suggests that those clearing the trees are in a sad state of mind. Curtis moves *sadly* to the beginning of the sentence: "Sadly, the trees are being cleared for farmland." This sentence stresses the point that it is sad to see the trees being cleared.
transitions—the bridges between parts of a sentence, between sentences, or between paragraphs; transitions enable the reader to make logical connections between ideas and carry a thought through for cohesiveness	The ninth-grade English class is learning about text types, and specifically about cause-and-effect and compare-and-contrast text structures. The students are given lists of transition words that support each type of text structure, such as *because*, *as a result*, *similarly*, *just like*, *however*, or *on the other hand*. Students work with partners to sort the transitions to distinguish which would work best for each text structure. Then, they practice writing sentences using these transition words.

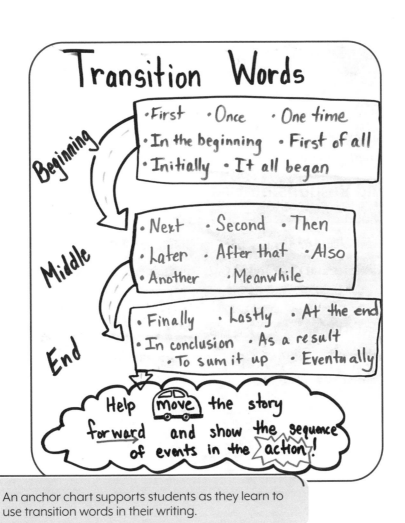

Transition Words

Beginning
- First   • Once   • One time
- In the beginning   • First of all
- Initially   • It all began

Middle
- Next   • Second   • Then
- Later   • After that   • Also
- Another   • Meanwhile

End
- Finally   • Lastly   • At the end
- In conclusion   • As a result
- To sum it up   • Eventually

Help move the story forward and show the sequence of events in the action!

An anchor chart supports students as they learn to use transition words in their writing.

Scrambled Sentences

Grades: K–1

Description

Students are given simple sentences with words written in an incorrect order and are asked to unscramble and rearrange the sentence parts.

Rationale

Start teaching students the parts of a sentence, and model sentence formation by having them identify and reorder parts of a sentence.

Roles and Responsibilities

Teacher: Model

- Guides students to identify parts of simple sentences.
- Provides cues and clues to help students remember sentence structures.
- Uses a variety of simple sentences for the exercise.

Student: Learner

- Identifies parts of simple sentences.
- Uses sentence strips to unscramble sentences.
- Practices orally before writing.

Process

1. Introduce or review parts of a sentence, including subject, verb, predicate, simple clauses, and punctuation.

2. Write out several simple sentences on strips, then cut the sentences apart to represent different parts of the sentence. On the back of each card, identify the part of the sentence.

3. Post sentence parts on sentence strips, and model how to combine sentence parts to create complete sentences. Think aloud to show how students can get hints from the backs of the cards.

4. Have students work with partners or in small groups at stations. Distribute the cut-up sentence strips to each station, and have students work together to arrange them into complete sentences. Students should discuss and orally practice each suggestion. Set a timer, and have each group rotate to a new station after five or ten minutes.

5. Follow up with independent work by providing sentences that are ordered incorrectly and asking students to rearrange them to create complete and correct sentences.

Differentiation

Color-code the cards to support formation, for example, subject words are written in red, verbs are in green. Create a poster of the color-code for reference. Model how to use other clues, such as capital letters and punctuation, as guides for the ordering of words in sentences. To increase complexity, remove all punctuation and ask students to insert capital letters and commas as needed. Gradually use more complex sentences for students to unscramble.

Sentence Expanding

Grades: 2–3

Description

Use specific prompts to help students expand their sentences to include more details.

Rationale

When writing, specific details help paint a picture for the reader. This strategy allows students to intentionally add details that will give more information to the reader, while keeping the writing smooth and fluent. Use this activity during content-area instruction to encourage students to use details from texts they are reading and to practice writing across the curriculum.

Roles and Responsibilities

Teacher: Model

- Reviews parts of a sentence.
- Creates question stems to support expanding sentences (e.g., *where, when, why, how*).
- Uses guided practice to gradually release responsibility to students.
- Encourages students to experiment with a variety of word placements to create the best flow.

Student: Writer

- Practices sentence expansion orally before writing.
- Participates in generating details.
- Asks clarifying questions.

Process

1. Tell students they can expand simple sentences by adding details that give more information to the reader. Remind students that good writing should answer questions for the reader, paint a clear picture for the reader, and use words that flow naturally.

2. Model by posting a simple sentence, such as *The boy played*. Tell students there are a few questions they can answer that will help them expand this sentence. First, they can answer the question "Where?" Have students make suggestions about where the boy may have played. Write *Where* on a sheet of chart paper, and post their ideas below. Remind students that the answer may be a specific location, like a room, or a place, like a playground; it could also be the name of a town or even a country.

3. Ask each student to fold a sheet of paper into four quadrants. Have students work with partners to create several new sentences that explain where the boy played. Ask students to share aloud and then write their favorite sentences in the top right quadrant. Label the quadrant *Where*.

4. Tell students another question they can answer that will expand their sentences is "When?" Explain that the answer could be represented as a specific time, a time of day, a date, a season, even a year. Post another chart paper with the title *When*, and add students' ideas. Have them label the top left quadrant of their papers *When*.

5. Ask students to work with different partners to share sentences that explain when the boy played. Have them write their favorites in the appropriate place on their papers.

6. Another question students can answer is "Why?" Explain how this information could be added as a clause or as an appositive: *Because he finished his homework,…* or *The boy, who had met a friend, played*. Ask students to brainstorm some responses to "Why," and post these on another sheet of chart paper. Then, have students share ideas with partners and write sentences on the bottom right quadrant.

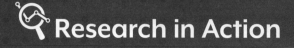

7. Finally, tell students they can also answer, "How did the boy play?" In this case, they will need to consider the verb *played*. Remind students that adverbs can be used, such as *energetically*. Another option is to use a comparison, such as *played like a kite dancing in the air*. Ask them to call out some suggestions. Post these on a fourth sheet of chart paper, labeled *How*. Have them work with other partners to generate ideas before adding sentences to the last quadrant on their papers.

8. Review students' sentences by asking them to share aloud. Use guiding questions to make corrections or suggestions to students, including asking about word order and which order sounds best when the sentence is read aloud. Have students experiment with moving words around so that they hear how clauses or adverbial phrases sound in different places in the sentence.

9. During content-area instruction, ask students to use this technique of answering the four questions to expand their sentences as they respond to reading in social studies, experiments in science, or problem-solving in math. Keep the chart paper visible, and add words or phrases that pertain to different subject areas as a reference.

Differentiation

Provide linking words, such as *because* or *so*, on sticky notes, and ask students to practice placing these in different locations within their sentences. Ask them how the meaning of the sentence changes when words are placed in different orders. Go further by having students edit their sentences for correct punctuation, including commas, dashes, or semi-colons. Use mentor texts to model sentences that provide just enough detail. Show students how adding too many details in one sentence can slow down the flow of reading and how to use punctuation to break up longer sentences.

Connectives

Description

Students practice using connectives within sentences and to combine sentences to add specific information to their writing.

Rationale

Similar to expanding sentences, connectives are the tools that help provide more detail in sentences. Connectives are the specific terms that students can choose when they want to add information, sequence ideas, highlight important information, explain why, explain a change, give an example, or demonstrate temporal situations. This activity shows how to use the right word or words to convey meaning.

Roles and Responsibilities

Teacher: Director

- Prepares a set of simple sentences written on strips, related to different content areas (mathematics, science, social studies).
- Provides charts showing connective words and examples of their use.
- Encourages collaboration through partner and small group work.

Student: Team member

- Distinguishes different kinds of details to add information to writing.
- Practices orally before writing.
- Experiments with placement of words to create compound, complex, and compound-complex sentences.

Research in Action

Process

1. Tell students that there are several distinct ways to add details to writing that provide specific information to the reader. Writers choose terms that will signify different kinds of details to the reader. For example, the writer may want to give an example or indicate a specific sequence of events. The writer chooses connective words that will help the reader understand the intention.

2. Post a chart showing specific connectives listed in columns. Label each column with one type of connective. Show connectives to support: *Adding Information* (such as *where, when,* or *how*), *Sequencing Ideas,* *Highlighing Important Information* (such as proper nouns, titles, specific academic terms), *Explaining Why, Showing Contrast* (such as *smaller than, better than*), *Giving an Example,* and *Showing Time.* (See example of connectives in figure 4.1 below.)

3. Write two or three simple sentences on the board. Think aloud and model how to use different connectives from each column to add different kinds of information. Have students work with partners through guided practice to add information to simple sentences in the same way.

4. Ask students to work in small groups at stations. Distribute a set of sentence strips and several sheets of paper to each station. The sentence strips should contain simple sentences pulled from content-area text, with any connective words removed. For example, for science, the sentences may read, "Plants take in oxygen. The sun provides light. Plants get food. Photosynthesis is a process. Plants give off carbon dioxide." Use sentences that describe a scientific phenomenon, a mathematical concept, or sentences that explain a historical event.

5. Explain to students that they will work with their groups to add connectives to the sentences to make cohesive paragraphs. Assign roles, such as recorder, presenter, and time-keeper. Tell them they will have a set amount of time to put the sentences into a logical order and to add connectives to make complete paragraphs. Have students practice adding connectives orally before writing anything on one of the sheets of paper. Remind them that

some connectives may fit in several columns, so they should be prepared to explain their choices.

6. After time is up, have groups mix up their sentence strips and rotate to another station and repeat the process. Have each group keep their sheet of paper and take it with them to the next station.

7. As a group, students should be able to justify the choices they made by explaining what kind of information they wanted to add to the sentences. For example, if they wanted to show sequence, then they chose connectives such as *first*, *next*, or *last*; or if they wanted to explain a cause and effect, then they chose connectives such as *therefore*, *since*, or *as a result*. Have one student from each group serve as the presenter to explain why they chose certain connectives.

8. For independent practice, have students experiment with the placement of the connectives within sentences and between sentences. Ask students to share their sentences with partners and discuss how the meanings changed when the words were reordered.

Differentiation

Give students smaller versions of the Sample Connectives Chart (figure 4.1 below), with space for them to add more examples as they come across them during reading, to save as mentor sentences for their own writing. Write connectives on small cards, with the word on one side and an example sentence or description of when to use it on the other. Have students keep the cards on rings as a reference when they write. Ask students to highlight connectives in their reading, using color coding to identify how and why it is used. Discuss how the author chose connectives specifically for different text structures depending on the purpose of the text.

Figure 4.1—Sample Connectives Chart

Add Information	Sequence Ideas	Highlight Important Information
Conjunction	first	…the one who
and	next	…the numerator
but	last	…the divisor
also	then	…the reaction
moreover	after	…the era
with	before	…the system
Where		
within		
next to		
beside		
When		
until		
as		
at the same time		
How		
happily		
reluctantly		
nervously		

Explain Why	Show Contrast	Give an Example	Show Time
since	more than…	for example…	before
therefore	smaller than…	this shows…	after
because	worse	as evidenced by…	until
so	better		soon
for this reason	stronger		subsequently
	higher		
	slower		

Sentence Mime

Secondary Grades

Description

Students annotate a piece of writing to identify types of sentence structures and syntax. Then, they write their own sentences that mimic these structures.

Rationale

Using mentor text allows students to practice writing in styles that are not familiar to them so that they may play with language and try out different text structures. Recognizing sentence structures and syntax helps students understand an author's purpose as they see the use of different structures as choices informed by content. Use this activity multiple times to introduce and practice one or two sentence structures at a time.

Roles and Responsibilities

Teacher: Facilitator

- Selects mentor texts from multiple content areas and time periods that represent different writing styles.
- Thinks aloud to demonstrate how to analyze and annotate text.
- Uses direct instruction and guided practice to gradually release responsibility to students.
- Follows up with mini-lessons on punctuation and grammar.

Student: Scribe

- Annotates text to identify sentence structures.
- Discusses ideas orally before writing.
- Practices mimicking sentences to gain understanding of word choice and syntax and their impact on the reader.

Research in Action

Process

1. Tell students that they will be practicing writing in the style of another author. Explain that there are many choices authors make, including sentence length, sentence patterns, and sentence structures.

2. Define the qualities of sentence length: sentences may be telegraphic, short, medium, or long. Provide text examples of each, and ask students to annotate with their own commentaries about the impact of each type of sentence. Have them share their annotations with partners.

3. Ask them to practice turning telegraphic sentences into medium sentences or long sentences into several short sentences. Have them describe their takeaways from this process.

4. Define different sentence patterns, such as declarative, imperative, interrogative, or exclamatory. Provide text examples of each, and ask students to annotate with their own commentaries about why a sentence pattern was used. Have them share their annotations with partners.

5. Ask students to practice creating each type of pattern using one simple sentence as a starter. Have them share their sentences with partners.

6. Continue in this manner to introduce and practice with other sentence structures and devices, such as balanced sentences, parallel structures, repetition, or use of complex and compound-complex sentences. In each case, have them define the qualities of the device and then annotate mentor text to identify the structure or device and explain its effect on the reader.

7. Provide a prompt that relates to current content-area instruction. Ask students to write a response using at least two of the sentence types they have learned. Have them share their drafts with partners to see if their partners can distinguish the choices they made and why they made them.

8. Ask students to reflect on the purpose of reading different types of texts and writing in different styles.

Differentiation

In language arts, show how different sentence patterns and structures are used in poetry versus prose, and ask students to describe the effect of each form. In mathematics or science, ask students to write using a nontraditional form or style. Ask them to explain why certain styles of writing are more conducive to different content areas. Use a shared online document to allow students to comment on each other's drafts in real time. For ongoing practice, periodically highlight sentences in student work, and ask them to change these to another sentence structure, length, or style.

Research in Action

Mentor Texts

Description

Use mentor texts as models of different sentence lengths, sentence patterns, and sentence structures. Students practice writing in the style of another author to learn how to rearrange words and use language in different ways.

Rationale

Students need models as they learn to write. Copying the style of another text shows them that they have many options when they write their own original works. Gradually, they learn that different styles can be used to achieve different effects, and they can begin to make intentional choices about the syntax they use to express their ideas.

Roles and Responsibilities

Teacher: Facilitator

- Defines the text structure, sentence pattern, or other syntactical elements of the text.

- Thinks aloud to model how to annotate text.

- Encourages discussion before writing.

- Prepares mini-lessons on punctuation or specific grammatical functions as needed.

Student: Scribe

- Annotates text to find examples of model sentences.

- Discusses ideas orally before writing.

- Keeps examples of different sentence types and structures as references for their own writing.

Process

- **Grades K–1:** Select accessible texts from picture books. Identify one sentence type that students will be able to mimic. Have them practice writing their own versions of stories using only that sentence style.

- **Grades 2–3:** Choose excerpts from chapter books, including nonfiction texts across content areas. Have students identify sentence length and sentence structures, and ask them to find examples in their mentor texts. Then, ask students to each write a paragraph using these structures.

- **Grades 4–5** can use more diverse mentor texts, such as newspaper articles, speeches, or advertisements. Define sentence patterns in the context of task, audience, and purpose. Ask students to identify the choices the authors made and the impact those choices have on the reader. Use creative products that allow students to demonstrate different sentence types, such as creating a commercial, writing a social media post, or commentating on a sporting event. Ask students to explain how different syntactical choices change the writing.

- **Secondary** students can be exposed to more complex texts, including poetry, essays, and research reports. In addition to defining and identifying different text structures, ask students to combine multiple sentence types and patterns in their writing. Have them use text structure or tone to justify placement of long and short sentences, interrogative or exclamatory patterns, and varied sentence structures. Provide multiple opportunities to revise writing, adding or changing sentences as students become more adept and fluent with these styles.

Differentiation

In language arts, identify or color-code the parts of the sentence, including subject, verb, predicate, direct object, and clauses. Have students practice manipulating parts of a sentence orally first to hear how sentences sound before writing. Revisit sentence structures during mathematics, science, or social studies instruction, and refer back to the definitions and models from language arts. Call out the different types of texts and the different purposes they serve so students gain syntactical awareness.

Moving Forward: Top Must-Dos

Explicit teaching of writing sentences is foundational to good writing. These are the building blocks that enable students to be fluent and proficient writers. "As students write, they learn by doing. They try out different forms of writing, apply different strategies and approaches for producing text, and gain fluency with basic writing skills such as handwriting, spelling, and sentence construction" (International Literacy Association 2020, 3). Revising writing to be more cohesive, more complex, and more interesting exerts a cognitive load that requires some level of automaticity in sentence construction. Therefore, it is imperative that students be given opportunities to explore sentence creation at the most basic levels and to gradually increase their abilities to create more complex structures.

For early grades, simply identifying nouns and verbs will impress upon students the need for sentences to be about *something* and to include an *action*. As students advance through elementary school, they can learn techniques for adding more detail to their simple sentences and then learn ways to combine or rearrange sentences and sentence components to change emphasis or to impact meaning. By the time they reach secondary school, students should have achieved comfort with a variety of rehearsed sentence structures. "Deliberate practice of skills in the primary grades sets the stage for training in secondary education, which in turn sets the stage for training in college" (Kellogg and Whiteford 2009, 257).

Teach the Way Words Work in Sentences

We cannot assume that simply reading well-crafted sentences will translate into an understanding of how to craft these sentences, just as watching a basketball game does not translate into being a basketball player. Students need explicit instruction each step of the way, which means breaking writing down to its component parts. This may seem intuitive in language arts, where descriptive words, action verbs, and use of transitions are inherent in the texts students read and study. In mathematics, consider showing how appropriate verbs and exact mathematical terminology help paint a clearer picture for the reader of how to solve the problem. In science, call out the transition words that indicate process steps, and in social studies, pay attention to how pronouns and temporal words help keep track of people and events.

Model, Explore, and Gradually Release

Students need multiple opportunities to combine "sentences into the more complex pattern until they can do this correctly and easily. They should be encouraged to use newly mastered sentence construction skills when writing and revising text" (International Literacy Association 2020, 9). Gradual release underscores the value of mentor text, as the teacher can demonstrate how sentence construction looks when successfully completed by other authors. Then, the teacher can think aloud to model the step-by-step process that a writer goes through. By making students responsible for one small piece of sentence construction at a time, they are more likely to experience success which will increase their comfort level when asked to try something more challenging. "Studying models of effective texts that can be imitated in their own writing…offers an alternative way to enhance not only individual sentence construction, but also establishing cohesive links among sentences" (Kellogg and Whiteford 2009, 257). In the elementary grades, demonstrate sentence construction and sentence combining in the context of content-area instruction so students see the relevance of the skill. When taken out of context, students may not be able to readily transfer the skill they practiced in an authentic way.

> By making students responsible for one small piece of sentence construction at a time, they are more likely to experience success which will increase their comfort level when asked to try something more challenging.

Teach Parts of a Sentence

For younger students, start with sentence parts and give plenty of practice opportunities, particularly across all content areas. "Constructing written sentences is a complex process involving decisions about word choice, syntax, textual connections, clarity, and rhythm. A limited knowledge about how to construct written sentences diminishes students' success in translating their thoughts into text…

Teaching students how to construct written sentences reduces grammatical miscues, increases sentence complexity, and results in qualitatively better text" (International Literacy Association 2020, 8). Students of all ages need to be familiar with basic sentence construction rules so that their writing is easy to read and understand. Encourage students to practice reading their writing aloud so they can learn to hear when a sentence "sounds awkward." If they never hear well-constructed sentences, how will they know the difference? Require students of all ages to always respond to you and others in complete sentences, and provide enough scaffolds in the way of sentence frames and stems to give them plenty of practice with different sentence structures and word combinations.

Practice Sentence Formation and Revision in All Content Areas

Call out examples frequently in mentor text, including nonfiction and content-specific examples. "As students practice producing specific types of written sentences, they gain familiarity and facility with the syntactical structures underlying each of them. This increased recognition of sentence patterns allows students to process information in similar sentences they are reading more quickly" (International Literacy Association 2020, 8). Revisiting activities such as Expanding Sentences or Using Connectives will increase fluency and flexibility for young writers and reiterate that writing is a skill that is important in all content areas, not just language arts. In secondary grades, a mathematics or science teacher should not think of themselves as taking on the responsibility of language arts instruction; rather, they should consider how students are able to access the textual content of their discipline and how they are able to best express their understanding of the curriculum in writing. Calling attention to the unique sentence patterns and structures of the content area directs students' thinking and helps them process information more effectively.

Further Considerations

Avoid practicing sentence formation and revision strategies only during reading or language arts. Studies show that typically, students receive less than one hour of writing instruction each day, most of which takes place in the language arts arena. In "Changing How Writing Is Taught," Steve Graham addresses the inadequacies of traditional writing instruction; that is, teacher preparation and instructional time, among other factors. Graham asserts that while "a majority of…middle and high school teachers in the investigations…used writing to support learning across the disciplines, most of the writing activities applied for this purpose involved writing without composing (e.g., filling in blanks on a work sheet, note taking, and one-sentence responses to questions)" (2019, 279). If students are to value writing as a means of expressing knowledge as well as a form of effective communication, all teachers across all content areas must provide opportunities to write and give students strategies for crafting and revising their work. This may require additional training for teachers and a shared professional commitment from schools and districts.

My Teaching Checklist

Are you ready to develop students' abilities to construct stronger and more interesting sentences and paragraphs? Use this checklist to help you get started!

Revise for Purpose: Syntax of Sentences and Beyond

Look Fors	Description
Explicit and systematic instruction in sentence formation and syntactical awareness is provided.	• Break down instruction into foundational skills. • Use a variety of mentor texts as models.
Responsibility is gradually released to students.	• Break down processes into simple steps, and practice one step at a time until a level of mastery is achieved. • Include guided practice opportunities so students can share orally before writing. • Use regular, ongoing formative assessments to immediately address misconceptions.
Syntax and language support are provided.	• Use scaffolds such as sentence stems, word banks, and charts to set an expectation of proficiency. • Students can always go above and beyond the scaffolds as they become more confident. • Frequently offer examples from mentor texts across the curriculum to emphasize the role of writing in all disciplines.

Chapter Summary

Breaking down a process to its component parts seems to come more naturally to teachers of some grade levels and subjects. In early elementary grades, teachers understand that their young students can only manage one or two skills at a time. In sports or music, the coach or the teacher recognizes the need for continued practice of discrete skills before combining those skills and ultimately using the skills authentically. Writing instruction also depends upon these processes. While students may have plenty of ideas to express, if they do not have specific skills, their ideas will be confined by the limits of their understanding of language. The consistent expectation of complex and appropriate syntax gives students a means to be subtle, nuanced, and deliberate. Syntax allows students to make distinctions between shades of meaning and levels of emphasis. Students can expect to be more clearly understood and can more clearly express their own understanding. Explicit attention to sentence formation, including sentence parts, sentence patterns, and sentence structures, is vital to this endeavor. Use of gradual release stresses the importance of ongoing practice and mastery learning. And shared responsibility among all content-area teachers shows students that language is the currency of knowledge, no matter the discipline.

Reflection Questions

- How often do students revisit their own writing? What are some ways to break down writing instruction into more discrete skills?

- What kind of writing activities are students asked to complete across content areas?

- How often are students asked to share orally before writing? What do those discussions look like?

Chapter 5

Grammar, Usage, and Mechanics

Background Information and Research

Chances are, when you think of grammar, you think of a set of specific rules for word placement, verb tenses, and subject-verb agreement. Perhaps you were taught how to diagram sentences and identify parts of speech. Or you may never have received any formal grammar instruction and instead have always relied on an intuitive sense of what "sounded right" when you spoke or wrote.

Historically, grammar instruction focused on "correct" usage of the English language. This prescriptive definition aimed to standardize language rules but ultimately stigmatized those with specific dialects or others who did not have the benefit of formal education. It was a "mistaken belief that grammar lessons must come before writing, rather than grammar being something that is best learned *through* writing" (Cleary 2014, para. 4). Today, research promotes an asset-based pedagogy in which students are taught that there are different ways of speaking and writing which may be appropriate for different purposes and different audiences. Grammar is not so much about what is "correct" but more about what order of words or types of sentence construction will best convey the thoughts and ideas of the author. Grammar should be taught within context. It should be addressed as part of the writing process, through drafting, editing, and revising, while the writer is examining the content of the text and making thoughtful decisions about organization and shades of meaning.

Connection to the Rope

Considering these recommendations in conjunction with Scarborough's Reading Rope (2001) and thinking of how students develop as readers and writers, grammar is one of the comprehension strands that requires explicit strategy instruction. This connection encourages teachers to consider appropriate strategies as they "determine the best instruction to help...learners succeed" (VanHekken 2021, para. 14). Translated to writing, elements such as critical thinking and syntax become the justifications for focusing on the recursive writing process and for considering "the way in which we order words in order to create sentences that follow conventional grammatical rules" (Smarten Up 2021, para. 5).

What is the best strategy, then, for integrating grammar into the curriculum? Gartland and Smolkin recommend three principles for grammar instruction:

1. Integrate grammar into the overall language arts curriculum.

2. Develop clear objectives for grammar instruction.

3. Experiment with different classroom activities (2016, 393–394).

Implications for Teaching and Learning

First, grammar instruction should be integrated into all aspects of the curriculum. Grammar should be taught in the context of reading, writing, and speaking. "An integrated approach to grammar instruction, where learning about grammatical concepts is taught through reading and authentic writing activities, is a much better approach to teaching grammar. Students who are taught with an incorporated approach are better able to apply advanced grammatical constructions to their own writing, and their writing also tends to be more error-free" (Harrity 2012, 24). With this organic infusion, students adjust their syntax in real time, not so much for the purpose of catching errors but for the purpose of clarifying meaning. "Teachers need to be in tune to the pace at which each of their students' writing is developing and individualize grammar instruction based on their needs" (24). This can be achieved across content-area instruction as students practice sentence construction both orally and in writing. Teachers should provide frequent opportunities for speaking and listening, as well as contextual reading, so students can practice seeing, hearing, and using diverse sentence structures. Ask students to speak in complete sentences, provide stems and frames, and challenge them to incorporate more complex sentences in their daily discourse. Not only will their grammar improve,

> Grammar is not so much about what is "correct" but more about what order of words or types of sentence construction will best convey the thoughts and ideas of the author.

but they will also gain more access to their content-area text as they become more comfortable with different text types and patterns. "A byproduct is…content improvement, particularly when teachers help students make connections between authors' grammatical choices and meaning through engaging activities" (Gartland and Smolkin 2016, 397).

Instruction should also include thoughtful objectives. Develop clear objectives for grammar instruction so that it becomes an intentional part of the lesson, rather than an accidental diversion. When developing the content objectives for a unit or lesson, consider the responses students will be expected to give. Are there ways to ensure that students provide more than just simple sentences or brief fill-in-the-blank answers? We want students to understand how language works and how to use language to effectively, appropriately, and accurately relay meaning. "[G]oals for writing need to focus on using writing for real purposes and writing in a more realistic fashion (e.g., access to source material, engaging in critical thinking)" (Graham 2019, 288).

One way to infuse this instruction is to ask students to cite text evidence and to mimic the writing styles of the authors they are studying. Students can spend time recognizing verb tenses and show how these relate to the conceptual understanding of events in history or experiments in science. Teachers can also demonstrate how changing the order of words in a prompt can impact the problem-solving steps of a mathematical calculation. "One reason why schools need to place more emphasis on writing is that it enhances students' performance in other important school subjects" (Graham 2019, 284). When students have a clear understanding of how language can be manipulated to convey meaning, they have more power to make conscious choices about how they express their thoughts and ideas, and they improve academically across content areas. "[T]asks like responding to a text in social studies or writing descriptions of natural phenomena in science class can provide more writing practice for students. Increasing the amount of writing in the content areas can be a way to deepen content-area learning while expanding writing activities" (Coker et al. 2016, 31).

> " Increasing the amount of writing in the content areas can be a way to deepen content-area learning while expanding writing activities.
>
> —David Coker et al. (2016, 31) "

Finally, take every opportunity to focus on language through fun and engaging oral and written activities. Try using a variety of instructional approaches for teaching grammar. Students need to feel safe experimenting with language. They need to be free to make mistakes. Leave the rule-bound, non-contextual worksheets behind, and instead dive into exercises and strategies that are explicitly linked to the students' own work. Capitalize on group work, collaboration opportunities, and even games or competitions to make the learning more verbal and interactive. Let them practice grammar authentically with their own discourse. "In grammar instruction, the goal is not to teach grammar rules but to teach how to apply them in language skills…. Unless learners know how to apply grammatical concepts in language skills, knowledge of grammar will not be useful" (Mart 2013, 4).

Activities should include plenty of modeling, guided practice, and ongoing feedback. In fact, research supports grammar interventions happening in the moment on a case-by-case basis. "Teachers must be willing to commit to providing quality writing instruction and they must afford the students multiple opportunities during the week to write as well as provide them with constructive feedback to ensure that they understand their writing errors and are able to make corrections using the strategies they learn during writing instruction" (Robinson and Feng 2016, 14). "Students acquire knowledge and beliefs about how to write through mentoring, feedback, collaboration, and instruction" (Graham 2019, 286), so it is important to provide multiple opportunities for grammar discussions through varied activities. "Immersing students in authentic reading and writing activities, using mini-lessons to teach grammatical concepts, and showing applied grammatical concepts in real life leads to better student writing" (Harrity 2012, 25).

More than anything, do not let grammar instruction become drudgery for students. Contextualizing the grammar instruction is more motivating than teaching it as a separate skill so that students "view writing as something that can be enjoyable, rather than something that causes them anxiety because they might do it wrong" (Giordano 2018, para. 9). Continue to reinforce that writing is a process and that grammar is just one more small adjustment that can help students be more nimble writers and more precise communicators.

Key Terms for Teacher Understanding

The following chart provides definitions of essential terms educators need to know and an example of each one.

Term and Definition	Example
active/passive voice—*active voice* means that a sentence has a subject that acts upon its verb; *passive voice* means that a subject is a recipient of a verb's action	Makena's sixth-grade class is asked to write letters to the mayor asking for a skate park to be added to the recreation center. Makena's teacher returned her letter with comments to use active voice, since this was a persuasive piece of writing and active voice is stronger. Makena asked her teacher for an example, and her teacher showed her one sentence that read, "Skating is done by kids of all ages." She said this was passive voice because the subject (*kids*) was being acted upon (*skating*). To change it to active voice, Makena wrote, "All kids skate." Now, the subject (*kids*) does the action (*skate*).
edit—the stage of the writing process when changes are made to ensure the writing adheres to the conventions of written English, including grammar, spelling, word choice, punctuation, and formatting	After Asad reads about the importance of rivers to civilization, he composes a cause-and-effect paragraph. In his draft, he cites information about how rivers support irrigation, commerce, and travel. His teacher gives him comments, and his tablemate also peer edits his paragraph. Then, he makes changes based on their suggestions and writes a final copy with the edits included.

(Continued)

Term and Definition	Example
grammar, usage, and mechanics—*grammar* is the structure of written or spoken language, the parts of speech, and how they combine to form sentences; *usage* is the way words and phrases are used to produce coherent sentences; *mechanics* refers to conventions of written language, such as capitalization, punctuation, and spelling	Tomas and his partner Julia added ice to two cups—one filled with plain water and one filled with salt water. They noticed that the ice melted faster in the plain water. As they collaborate to write up an explanation of the phenomena, they discuss what they think happened. Tomas records their conversation as notes in his science notebook, but before they write up a draft to turn in, they each review the notes to check for readability. Julia edits for punctuation and spelling, and Tomas pays attention to the verb tense and subject-verb agreement. They read it aloud as they write to check their grammar.
participle—a type of word derived from a verb that is used for a variety of purposes, such as an adjective or to construct verb tenses. For regular verbs, a *past participle* is typically formed by adding *–ed* to the end of the root form of a verb. *Present participles* are formed by adding *–ing* to the root form of a verb.	Gustavo wrote, "We have to fix the fence because the dogs had jump over it." His writing partner told him the sentence did not sound right. Their teacher hears their conversation and does a mini-lesson on participles. Afterward, Gustavo changed his sentence to, "We had to fix the fence because the dogs were jumping over it."

Term and Definition	Example
subject/predicate—two parts of a sentence; the *subject* is what or whom the sentence is about, and the *predicate* is a clause that tells something about the subject, what it is doing, or a description about it	As Mr. Abbott introduces the math lesson, he gives the students a way to understand the prompt by underlining the subject and circling the verb. He tells students that the subject will help them know what to solve and the verb will tell them how to solve it. After the students work through an equation, he has them write a description of how they solved it. He reminds them that their opening sentences should contain the *subject* from the prompt and a *predicate* that includes a verb and a description of their first steps.
tense—the *tense* of a verb tells you when something existed or happened. There are three main tenses: present, past, and future. *Present* describes things that are currently happening; *past* describes things that have already happened; *future* refers to events that have not happened but that are due to happen.	Jackson is writing a story about a time he was brave. He wants to add a flashback to his story, so he stops using the past tense of verbs, such as *went*, *jumped*, *fell*, or *laughed*, and begins writing in present tense so that the reader feels like the flashback event is happening right now. He uses sentences such as, "I see the shiny red bike, and I jump on and pedal as fast as I can." As the story reaches the climax, Jackson adds a lesson learned that he can remember in the future. He uses a different verb tense and writes, "Next time, I will tie my shoes and I will look both ways."

Parts of Speech

adjective	a word that describes a noun or pronoun
adverb	a word that describes a verb, an adjective, another adverb, or a sentence and that is often used to show time, manner, place, or degree
article	any of a small set of words or affixes (such as *a*, *an*, and *the*) used with nouns to limit or give definiteness to the application
conjunction	a word that joins two grammatical elements of the same sentence or construction; words that illustrate the meaning between two clauses, such as *and*, *but*, or *or*
noun	a word that is the name of something (such as a person, animal, place, thing, quality, idea, or action) and is typically used in a sentence as a subject or object of a verb or as an object of a preposition
preposition	a word or group of words that is used with a noun, pronoun, or noun phrase to show direction, location, or time or to introduce an object
pronoun	a word (such as *I*, *he*, *she*, *you*, *it*, *we*, or *they*) that is used instead of a noun or noun phrase
verb	a word that shows an action (*sing*), occurrence (*develop*), or state of being (*exist*)

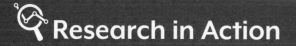

Picture Books

Grades: K–1

Description

Students create albums filled with pictures that are labeled to showcase verbs, nouns, and adjectives they encounter in their lives. Students use pictures they draw or images from stories or nonfiction texts.

Rationale

While knowing how to categorize nouns and verbs does not explicitly support writing, this activity builds understanding of language and how it works, and helps students develop rich vocabulary to better express themselves. At first, teachers may need to write captions for the pictures, but as students become more proficient, they gain ownership of different parts of speech as they label their pictures.

Roles and Responsibilities

Teacher: Facilitator

- Defines *noun*, *verb*, and *adjective* and posts definitions with examples.

- Provides pictures as models.

- Uses a graphic organizer to capture parts of speech, and posts examples of nouns, verbs, and adjectives as students encounter them.

Student: Investigator

- Practices labeling pictures orally before writing.

- Sorts pictures by parts of speech.

- Identifies images across content areas.

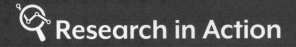

Research in Action

Process

1. Tell students they will be creating a collection of words which they will save in a special picture album.

2. Show several pictures or illustrations of people, pets, objects, toys, food, or locations, such as a park, a school, or a building. Tell students these are all *nouns*. Ask them to help you write a definition of a *noun*, and guide them to include *people*, *places*, and *things*. Have them tell their partners three other items that are nouns.

3. Show several pictures or illustrations of action words, such as *throwing*, *jumping*, *racing*, *climbing*, or *eating*. Tell students these are *verbs*. Ask students to help you define *verb*, and guide them to include *words that show action*. Have them think of three other verbs, and ask them to share with partners.

4. Show several pictures or illustrations of nouns that students can describe by their size, color, shape, or texture. Explain that these details are called *adjectives*. Ask students to help you define *adjective*, and guide them to include *words that describe a noun*. Have students think of three other adjectives, and have them share with partners.

5. Tell students it is their turn to collect nouns, verbs, and adjectives. Provide each student with several sheets of paper stapled or folded together or a blank notebook. Ask them to draw or find pictures from magazines or the internet that represent nouns, verbs, and adjectives. Have them sort the pictures and group them by their parts of speech. Then have students discuss their selections with partners.

6. Ask students to add the pictures to their notebooks. Tell them to identify the part of speech and to label each picture with a caption describing it. For example, students could write *ball* on a picture of a ball for the *noun* page, they could write *throw* on the picture for the *verb* page, or they could write *red ball* on the picture for the *adjective* page. Provide word cards or assist with writing the labels as needed.

7. Ask students to keep some pages empty, and explain that they can continue to add words and pictures to their albums as they encounter more examples. Recall this activity during mathematics, science, or social studies instruction, and ask students to record the nouns, verbs, and adjectives they find.

8. Ask a few students to share their albums with the class. Post labeled pictures around the room, and encourage students to add pictures and words to the posters.

Differentiation

Use word cards to help students write the labels and names of the pictures. Color-code nouns, verbs, and adjectives, and use colored construction paper as the album so students remember how to sort the words. Use this activity as a bell-ringer or as students line up to go outside, and have them keep adding to their collection of nouns, verbs, and adjectives. Use mnemonics or hand signals to help them remember the definitions.

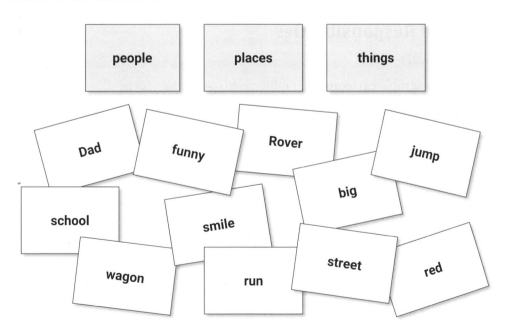

In Agreement: Cartoon Conversations

Grades: 2–3

Description

Students use storyboards to create cartoon conversations, which allows them to practice creating a succession of subject-verb sentences.

Rationale

Students can use real-life or text-based examples as models for their cartoon conversations and experiment with verb tense and verb agreement using a visual medium to support their understanding. Students will recognize that writing can represent speech and that similar rules apply to oral and written discourse. Use this activity during language arts or social studies as a means of representing a sequence of events.

Roles and Responsibilities

Teacher: Model

- Provides sample cartoons or graphic novels as mentor texts.
- Uses storyboard templates or online resources to create cartoons.
- Introduces common features of comics, such as speech bubbles, thought bubbles, and different shapes or icons to show action or emotion.

Student: Author

- Generates conversations between characters.
- Uses familiar stories or invents original stories.
- Practices with verb tense and verb agreement.

Process

1. Tell students they will be creating stories to practice writing sentences that contain a subject and verb.

2. Display a cartoon or graphic novel, and model reading the panels. Identify the parts of each sentence to show that each character uses a subject and a verb. Have students work with partners to identify subjects and verbs in additional panels.

3. Distribute a storyboard template to each student. Explain that each box will represent a scene from a familiar text. They will draw pictures of the characters having conversations that are pulled from the text. (Students may create original stories as well.)

4. Draw or create icons to represent speech bubbles, thought bubbles, and actions or emotions, and model how to include these on the storyboard.

5. Tell students each box should contain at least two speech bubbles to represent a conversation between the characters. Model by drawing two characters and using a speech bubble to show the character making a statement or asking a question, as well as a response from the second character. Remind students that each sentence should contain a subject and a verb, and redefine these terms if needed. Ask students to tell partners the definitions and to give an example of a sentence that one of the characters might say.

6. Have students create their first panels using pencils. Walk around to make sure students are including speech bubbles and that they are adding sentences that contain subjects and verbs.

7. As students continue to add panels to their storyboards, task them with using verbs that end in –*ing*. Ask, "Do verbs always end in –*ing*? What does this ending tell you about the action?"

8. In another panel, tell students to use verbs that end in –*s*. Ask, "What happens when you add –*s* to the end of a verb? How do you decide if a verb should end in –*s* or in –*ing*?"

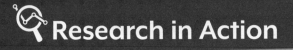

9. As students continue to add panels, ask them to identify if the action is taking place in the present or if they are describing past or future events. What changes will they need to make to the verbs in their sentences?

10. Ask students to explain how to write verbs when more than one person is doing the action. Show them different verb conjugations, or display examples of singular and plural verbs.

11. Have students share their comics with partners for peer editing, or collect comics and redistribute to the class. Provide a checklist so peers can validate that each sentence contains a subject and verb, that all verbs are representing the appropriate time (past, present, or future), and that verbs are either singular or plural depending on the subject of the sentence.

12. Have students make any corrections identified by their peers. Then, have each student create a final copy of their comic using markers.

Differentiation

Give students plenty of mentor texts so they see multiple examples. Have students create time lines or outlines before creating their panels so they can plan a draft of their stories. Have students use laminated templates of storyboards and dry-erase markers during guided practice as a way to do formative assessment while they practice writing sentences and using verbs. Use online storyboard tools or applications, and have students do this activity to summarize events from history or scientific discoveries.

Scavenger Hunt

Grades: 4–5

Description

Students receive a mini-lesson on a grammatical topic, then they use mentor texts to find examples of similar structures in content-area text. They now have added a variety of sentence structures to their writing repertoires and can demonstrate understanding by expanding their own writing to mirror the examples they have found in texts.

Rationale

By finding examples of grammar topics in content-area text, students are learning grammatical functions as an integrated part of the curriculum. Mini-lessons support connections between reading and writing and provide multiple examples of how word choice and word placement impact meaning.

Roles and Responsibilities

Teacher: Guide

- Prepares mini-lessons on grammar based on results of ongoing formative assessments.
- Finds mentor texts to showcase examples of sentence structures and patterns.
- Includes grammar and discourse in content-area objectives, along with writing activities to demonstrate learning.

Student: Writer

- Maintains journals and notebooks for writing across the curriculum.
- Practices sentence combining and sentence expanding as part of the revision process.
- Identifies grammatical choices during reading as a means of providing additional layers of meaning to content.

Process

1. Use formative assessments to determine areas of need for students, and plan mini-lessons within content-area instruction.

2. Identify a mentor text that shows either examples or non-examples of a specific grammatical structure. Help students identify the characteristics of the structure, including when and how it is used.

3. Have students annotate mentor text to find examples of similar structures within content-area text. Ask them to work with partners or in small groups to discuss the examples they found.

4. Ask students to practice writing similar sentences in an authentic writing assignment related to the content. See the examples below.

Examples

- **Social Studies:** Practice identifying pronouns in nonfiction text. Have students circle pronouns and then draw a line to the subject or noun to which they are referring. Ask why authors make choices to replace proper nouns with pronouns. Then, have students write summaries of historical events, and ask them to include at least five pronouns. Have them work with partners to connect the pronouns to a noun or subject in their own writing. Were there nouns that could be replaced with pronouns?

- **Mathematics:** Have students read a word problem and circle the verb(s). What is the problem asking them to do? What kind of verbs are used in mathematics? Create lists of verbs and demonstrate how they translate to mathematical operations. Next, identify the steps to solve the problem by simplifying the sentences. Cross out any extemporaneous information, and number the steps in the directions. What information remains? What details are missing? How can this information help you determine how to approach the problem? Once students have unpacked prompts, have them practice turning number sentences into written mathematical story problems. They should use appropriate verbs and give clear step-by-step directions. Then, have them share their word problems with partners to solve.

- **Science:** Give examples of adverbs and adjectives, and show how these parts of speech provide details that answer *when*, *how*, or *why* or that give specific descriptive details. Ask students why science especially requires very clear and precise descriptions. Use mentor texts, such as explanations of phenomena or descriptions of data, and have students cross out the adverbs and adjectives, then trade with partners. What information is missing when these words are removed? As students study a phenomenon or analyze data, ask them to write summaries and include specific adverbs and adjectives that provide more information, such as *when*, *how*, or *why*.

Differentiation

Use color-coding for different parts of speech, and have students highlight their own writing as they edit and revise. Provide instruction and practice on one element at a time, and use ongoing formative assessments to determine mastery. Revisit parts of speech in different content areas, and reiterate their functions and purposes. Use word cards to highlight conjunctions or connectives, and using sentence strips, have students practice combining and expanding sentences. Challenge students with specific criteria that must be included in each paragraph, such as *Paragraph 1 must contain two unique transition words* or *The closing paragraph must start with a prepositional phrase.* These constraints foster creativity as they require students to form more complex sentences.

Mini-Write, Mini-Lesson

Description

During content-area instruction, students read a portion of text and then write a response. Teachers can use this structure to address a variety of grammar functions through contextual mini-lessons using the gradual release model.

Rationale

Short writing assignments provide low-stakes practice opportunities. Students can gain proficiency or mastery by repeating a strategy and demonstrating a skill across content areas. This supports transfer of the skill and boosts students' confidence when writing for different purposes.

Roles and Responsibilities

Teacher: Model

- Finds multiple examples of mentor texts across disciplines.
- Uses student work as additional mentor examples.
- Thinks aloud and models one discrete skill at a time, using frequent checks for understanding at pivotal points in the lesson.
- Releases responsibility to students.

Student: Novice

- Writes every day to gain confidence.
- Recognizes writing as both a product and a means of learning.
- Reflects on own writing and sets realistic goals for improvement.

Process

1. Review student work to identify a grammar skill that is challenging for most students.

2. Create a set of process steps that students can follow for a mini-lesson that addresses the skill. For example, for a mini-lesson on subject-verb agreement, first identify the gap (e.g., students are using the wrong form of the verb); next, describe a strategy that will help students remember how to check for this error on their own (e.g., Is the subject about one thing or more than one thing? Write the number above the subject. If it is one thing, the verb must be singular. If it is more than one thing, the verb must be plural.); third, provide options for how to fix the error (e.g., look up verb conjugations or use premade charts as references).

3. Think aloud as you model the process steps, using a piece of authentic text from content-area reading or a student's exemplar. After demonstrating the steps once ("I do"), have students work with partners to repeat the process while you check for understanding after each step ("We do").

4. Have students use another piece of mentor text to work through the process together as you walk around, listen in, and make suggestions or corrections to students ("You try").

5. Finally, ask students to demonstrate the skill independently as they read a new piece of text on their own ("You do").

6. As students gain proficiency in the skill, tell them they need to demonstrate that specific skill as they read and respond to text. Give students a longer piece of text to read, and identify two or three places where they should stop and respond to a prompt about what they read. Tell students they must respond in complete sentences, and their responses should demonstrate the skill they just learned.

7. Include this process across content areas, using student progress to determine the skill that needs to be addressed.

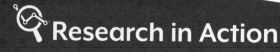

Differentiation

Continue to repeat skill practice in this way multiple times until it becomes habitual. The more often students revisit a process, including across content areas, the easier it becomes to internalize. Use student examples as mentor texts to showcase successful efforts and so that other students can feel validated. Find ways to embed skill building into the culture of the classroom. For example, devote a bulletin board to "bad grammar" that students find in the real world, in advertisements, newspaper articles, or even on social media. Show why grammar matters by finding examples of mistakes that impact meaning in a funny way, such as, *Tables are for eating customers only*. Challenge students to find more examples, and then ask them to rewrite these.

Tables Are for Eating Customers ONLY

Moving Forward: Top Must-Dos

Grammar matters, but not because student writing is "incorrect" without it. Rather, grammar allows students to express meaning more precisely, with more nuance, and with more variety to hold the reader's interest. Without a repertoire of varied sentence structures to choose from, students resort back to a series of simple sentences that do not convey depth of thought and that are repetitious and uninteresting for the reader. "Adding this type of grammar to children's repertoires can open the door to educational success and socioeconomic mobility" (Gartland and Smolkin 2016, 392). Too often, grammar has been taught out of context, as a set of arbitrary rules. "Teachers need to look at grammar instruction in a more constructivist way, where students discover concepts for themselves and construct their own knowledge about it. This will lead students to become more motivated about learning grammar, because they will see the payoffs in their writing assignments" (Harrity 2012, 9).

Integrating grammar across content-area instruction can be done through authentic writing assignments. For younger grades, lay a foundation by addressing parts of a sentence and encourage ongoing practice. Elementary students can play with sentence construction through creative assignments that highlight specific criteria for sentences. By the time students are in secondary school, they should have gained some confidence in their ability to use grammar as a means of adding depth and precision to their writing. These students can practice perfecting sentence construction through just-in-time mini-lessons that help them make small adjustments and practice with authentic tasks. "Grammar instruction is most effective when mini-lessons are taught that target specific errors in student writing. It has been strongly suggested by some researchers that this is the most beneficial way of helping students to improve their command for grammar in writing" (Robinson and Feng 2016, 6).

Explicitly Teach How Language Functions

We cannot take for granted that students have internalized the parts of speech and what they signify in oral or written communication. It cannot be assumed that students recognize the difference between a passive and active voice, and why one may be a more appropriate choice than the other, depending on the task, audience, and purpose. "It is not only important for a student to know what a passive construction is…but they must also understand how a passive construction changes the way information is presented" (Gartland and Smolkin 2016, 394).

Breaking down skills to these small component parts may seem tedious; in truth, you are giving students opportunities to feel safe and successful so they are willing to take risks and take on bigger challenges. "Teachers need to applaud students for trying something new, and students need to be offered more support on the topic in order to learn to use the new concepts correctly" (Harrity 2012, 24). Using the gradual release model makes student thinking visible as teachers model and then do frequent checks for understanding before asking students to work independently. Creating fun, gamified lessons lowers students' affective filter and gives them permission to try new structures or to make mistakes. "Teachers must learn to reconceptualize their thoughts towards errors in student writing. Many errors are due to students trying out new ways of writing. Students do not need to be discouraged from trying new ways of writing, which can happen when teachers simply mark the errors and give them a bad grade" (Harrity 2012, 24).

> Creating fun, gamified lessons lowers students' affective filter and gives them permission to try new structures or to make mistakes.

Incorporate Read-Alouds and Shared Reading

Use mentor text to show students authentic examples of different grammatical structures. Think aloud as you unpack the writing and surmise what choices the author made. Pause to discuss or point out conventions that the writer used, and discuss what these indicate. Ask questions, such as, "What punctuation is used during speaking? Why? What does this suggest about the tone or mood of the writing?" According to Cagri Mart (2013), grammar is more easily understood during conversation because when learners hear the words, the rules are easier to perceive. Students of all ages need many opportunities to see, hear, read, and discuss grammar in texts across the curriculum. Involve younger students in the read-alouds by having them work with partners or in small groups and listen for specific elements of sentence construction, such as use of pronouns or a good mix of simple, compound, and complex sentences. Older students can read excerpts of complex text and dissect the specific elements that contribute to tone or meaning.

Infuse Assessment

What do students need to know? What do students know already? What are they struggling with? Use assessment to drive instruction. Allow students to assess themselves with clear rubrics and expectations, and give them opportunities to revisit their work to make it better. "Students must receive feedback about their writing. They cannot be expected to learn anything from a simple marking up of all of the grammatical errors" (Harrity 2012, 8). These opportunities for feedback should be intentionally planned, which means the teacher needs to be clear about their objectives and expectations and be able to clearly communicate these to students. Students also need to take ownership of their learning by identifying the gaps in their own writing and by being willing to try new things to improve. Ask students to peer edit their classmates' work. Give them frequent opportunities to revise and resubmit writing, based on specific feedback.

Further Considerations

Avoid Teaching Grammar in Isolation

While grammar may traditionally have been taught as a unit or lesson apart from other content, exercises taught out of context do not help students transfer the skill to their own writing. "Grammar instruction needs to be thoughtfully integrated into the language arts curriculum" (Gartland and Smolkin 2016, 394), and in fact, integrated across all content areas. When students are shown ways to enhance meaning by strengthening their sentences, grammar takes on more relevance and importance. Error corrections on an activity sheet do not require as much cognitive work, nor is it meaningful for students. When they can apply grammar instruction to their own writing, students recognize the value of the skill. "In this way, students are learning grammatical concepts, but they are also learning how to use those grammatical concepts in writing and what effect different grammatical concepts can have on writing" (Harrity 2012, 19).

Limit Use of Grammar Worksheets

A worksheet represents a task that needs to be completed, rather than a skill that needs to be internalized. Students can quickly and sometimes effortlessly complete a grammar worksheet by looking for a pattern and simply replicating what they see. Worksheets do not contribute enough to working knowledge, nor do they provide a student with the flexibility to make choices based on meaning and intent. "Experienced professional writers have internalized a wide variety of syntactical resources from which they select to convey their thoughts and ideas" (Gartland and Smolkin 2016, 398). Our students need to learn to be experienced writers.

My Teaching Checklist

Are you ready to develop students' understanding of grammar, usage, and mechanics so they can become skilled writers? Use this checklist to help you get started!

Grammar, Usage, and Mechanics

Look Fors	Description
Explicit and systematic instruction in grammar, usage, and mechanics is provided.	• Teach for mastery, one skill at a time. • Base instruction on student need. • Embed mini-lessons across all content areas.
Responsibility is gradually released to students.	• I Do, We Try, You Try, You Do • Model with mentor texts. • Conduct intentional formative assessments at every stage. • Make just-in-time adjustments during instruction.
Rubrics are provided to support grammar usage.	• Include language objectives across the curriculum. • Be explicit about grammar expectations. • Instead of calling out errors, show how appropriate grammar impacts meaning.

Chapter Summary

This chapter emphasizes the need to move away from traditional grammar instruction that focuses on rules and conventions. Instead of grading students for the correctness of their sentences, show students how to make grammatical choices that can change or enhance the meaning they are trying to convey. This can be accomplished when grammar is taught in context, throughout the curriculum, in response to student need. Include grammar objectives during content-area instruction, and call out language structures in rubrics and assessments. Help students feel comfortable with the revision process through varied activities that make it fun to try new language structures. Encourage students to try something new, even if they make a mistake, because that is a more authentic way to learn. Be patient. It takes time to develop enough skills in sentence construction to be nimble and flexible, and students may need to practice many times before they feel confident in their abilities.

Reflection Questions

- What is your own comfort level with grammar? Is there a strategy that is helpful to you as a writer?

- How do you identify language objectives during your content-area instruction?

- Where can you insert intentional breaks to check for understanding and assess students' mastery?

- By what means will you identify the needs of your students when it comes to grammar and sentence construction?

Chapter 6

A Better Way: Micro Writing

by Kim Carlton
Richardson, Texas

From the Classroom

At the start of the annual research paper assignment, I asked students to develop their own research goals. Walking the room, I saw notebooks and planners out as students jotted due dates. Andrew did not budge. He wrote nothing. When I stopped by to see his plan, he flatly responded, "I have never turned in a single research paper in 11 years of school."

Assuming, like all young teachers do, that I can solve any problem with just a few magic words, "Well, what happens each year on the due date?"

"I just don't come to school. Eventually, you guys just quit asking me about it. Writing is the worst. I always feel bad about it. It is easier to just not do it."

In this moment, I realized that there had to be a better way to get my students writing.

Using Small Writing for a Big Impact

We have all been where Andrew is, with a task that is so large it becomes a many-headed serpent needing to be slayed. Maybe it was the garage that needs cleaning, the weight you want to lose, or the degree you have always been planning to finish. When a task is too big, it feels impossible to start. So, like Andrew, you might feel bad about it and avoid it entirely.

Improving writers is like that garage that never gets clean. It is hard to tell where to start or when you are finished. There is always more work to do. To improve writing, students need to build vocabulary, develop well-crafted ideas, write with subject-verb agreement, and use punctuation. Each one of these skills is a box of stuff in this metaphorical garage. We might opt to skip teaching writing because the task is too big. We spend our time maneuvering around the stuff in the garage, feeling guilty as we do. But as teachers, we can move one box.

Why Micro Writing?

> Micro writing—a small burst of the writing process in the form of sentences or short paragraphs; can provide students with the necessary practice of the writing process, giving them small writing wins and the opportunity for quick and relevant feedback. Micro writing is a strategy to get students writing and revising without overwhelming them with the process.

Micro writing starts with short bursts of writing based on a stimulus. But micro writing moves beyond quick writes or freewriting. With micro writing, we take students through the entire writing process, using just sentences or a paragraph. They practice a small piece of writing and a small writer's revision, then reflect on the impact of that change. Students get a small win: a great sentence that has been through the writing process. And one good sentence makes for another and another and another. Moving prewriting to the next stage of the writing process is important. As Penny Kittle (2008) warns, "as seriously as I take freewriting in notebooks, I take just as seriously the need to move beyond it."

Talk It Out and Write It Down: Small Writing

Micro writing starts with a topic. Students could be responding to something they have read, heard, or viewed. They could ponder their own experiences or universal questions. These writing topics can be extended to create something larger and more formal, or the topic can be something just for this moment. Forming the prompt as a question makes the first sentence easy: all you have to do is answer it, and you are off to the races.

Sample Topics

- Should we abolish the penny? (persuasive)
- Why is fast-fashion a problem? (informative)
- Why is it important to try new things? (narrative)

Giving students two to four minutes, have them chat with partners about the topic. This should be more of a conversation. It is thinking before they write. This conversation serves as verbal prewriting, allowing students to connect thought and language. You might collect a few groups' responses on an anchor chart to provide students with ideas, pertinent vocabulary, and an active word wall for writing.

The next step is to write it down. I give students just two to four minutes to draft their thoughts on the topic. As a practical matter, I try not to post the timer for this stage as I have found it causes more anxiety than motivation. Additionally, if I give students a small portion of paper, say a notecard or large sticky note, I have found that students are more likely to write. The terror of the blank page is real, and micro writing should be about nonthreating writing opportunities. You can always tape that small paper micro writing onto a larger sheet of paper to provide more space for the next steps: revision and editing.

Refine the Idea: Small Revision

If we only ask students to revise lengthy, major assignments, they do not practice the skill of revision frequently enough to be comfortable with it. Without revision, writing withers on the page. With revision, micro writing moves prewriting into something more. And while prewriting and freewriting are important, Penny Kittle reminds us, "collecting a lot of…first-thinking entries are not in and of themselves going to improve writing, or not enough anyway" (2008).

> "Revision, or reseeing, is not necessarily a natural act. It draws on a different source of energy, the energy of anticipation.
> —Donald Graves (1983, 160)"

Students should practice revision in lower-stakes situations and learn how revision can help writers refine ideas and play with language. In classrooms, the task of revision becomes overwhelming and reserved for only the finest of pieces. However, small revision done on small pieces of writing allows us the opportunity to clarify and narrow our teaching, practice, and feedback.

Taking the micro writing students have just completed, decide on one item for students to refine. I am using the word *refine* here since this step can blur the lines between revision and editing. Your refinement might encompass an editing skill, a revision technique, or maybe something in between. I try not to get too caught up in the naming conventions since often revision requires editing and vice versa. The trick to this stage is to pick just one area of focus that can improve writing quickly and completely.

Sample Ideas for Refining Micro Writing

- Eliminate 10 percent of the words. → Focus on word choice, wordiness, and redundancy.

- Find two sentences to combine into one. → Focus on syntax and sentence variety.

- Extend a sentence with a conjunction. → Focus on adding details. (Also incorporated here is editing for run-on sentences and preventing comma splices!)

Give students two to four minutes to refine their writing. Mill about to answer questions and collect great examples to share when the time ends. Students should be confident in entering this stage, having all the information they need to make these refinements. If you are focusing on combining sentences, then grab that anchor chart from the lesson where you previously taught it. If you are focusing on capitalization, take a few extra minutes to review the ways authors use capital letters. With a single, focused skill, you can provide the focused teaching to support it. Remember, you aren't teaching all the grammar and mechanics here, just one small thing.

TALK *it out.*

WRITE *it down.*

REFINE *the idea.*

REFLECT *on it.*

Reflect on It: Small Feedback

One of the benefits of micro writing is that the process creates a space for immediate feedback. Students need writing feedback. If you have spent any time in a class of writers, it is filled with waving hands pleading, "Miss, can you read this?" Research will say that feedback that is "timely, specific, understandable, and actionable" is best to help "students assimilate the language used by the teacher into their own self-talk" (Fisher, Frey, and Hattie 2016, 100). When the only feedback for writing comes from an assignment returned weeks after it was written, the impact of feedback is dismissed, and many times, ignored entirely.

Feedback can be provided to each student as they complete their micro writing. Grading 30 notecards of writing focusing on a single skill is far faster than responding to 30 papers. Walking the room with a clipboard while looking over shoulders immediately informs instruction and allows you to provide feedback and clarify misconceptions. At this stage of micro writing, feedback can also take the form of individual comparison, peer-to-peer sharing, or a full-class discussion. Let's look at an example shared as a full class:

> **Me:** Can someone share a change you made to your writing?
>
> **Student:** I first wrote, "The penny is useless." Then I added, "The penny is useless, and most people won't even stop to pick it up."
>
> **Me:** So, in your first draft, you have a declarative sentence, and in your second draft, you revised it with a conjunction and made a compound sentence by adding a new idea.
>
> *(See how we used our academic language to describe what the student did as a writer?)*
>
> **Me:** How did that improve your writing?
>
> **Student:** Well, you don't just have to take my word for it now. I gave you an example that everyone understands. I mean, do you pick up pennies?
>
> **Me:** What a great point! So, by expanding your sentence with a conjunction, you added a specific detail in just the right place and strengthened your argument by giving a real-world example.
>
> *(See how we showcased this revision and this writer's technique as something you can use when writing any piece?)*

Regardless of the method of feedback, it is important for students to pause, pull the pencils back, and look at the change they made and how it impacted their writing. This publishing phase of micro writing serves multiple purposes. We can reinforce that refining our writing makes writing better. We encourage students to practice a specific skill or technique and reflect on its impact. More broadly, sharing the changes to our writing—removing a word, adjusting a sentence, adding a detail—illustrates that revision and editing are beneficial acts that improve every writer's writing. Refining our writing after we write it isn't hard or daunting; it can be as simple as one small change. And this reflective thinking is an important final step to micro writing and to transferring the skill. "Think[ing] reflectively about the strategic thinking and action" gives students "internal scripts" they can follow for future writings (Fisher, Frey, and Hattie 2016, 101).

Small Wins

Writing is a series of choices. Some are big, such as topic, thesis, or structure, and some small, such as a single word or comma. And for students who struggle with writing, the concept of crafting a perfect essay feels so unattainable, they may not want to begin. With micro writing, students can see change and improvement immediately, with a small revision on a small amount of text. Writers can tinker with a word, a sentence, or even a punctuation mark and reflect on its impact on their writing when the amount of writing is small. Sharing that change and getting immediate feedback gives students a small win—the entire writing process in about ten minutes. Teresa Amabile and Steven Kramer, in their work *The Progress Principle*, discuss how a small win can "ignite joy, engagement and creativity" (2011b, 84).

> "Without the small wins, the big one likely won't happen—we give up in disappointment and frustration before we get to the big win. The small wins hold the key to momentum."
> —Jude King (2019, para. 8)

We all want to feel the thrill of a win. Research scientist Jude King says, "Without the small wins, the big one likely won't happen—we give up in disappointment and frustration before we get to the big win. The small wins hold the key to momentum" (2019, para. 8). In business and in the classroom, "every achievement—big or small—activates our brain's reward circuitry...which leaves us feeling energized, confident, and motivated." According to Amabile and Kramer, writing in the *Harvard Business Review*, "even ordinary, incremental progress can increase people's engagement in the work and their happiness" (2011a, para. 25).

For striving students, school doesn't offer many wins. And for students like Andrew, writing had become a winless game. We started micro writing that year in response to his avoidance of writing. Papers returned bleeding with ink didn't encourage him to write more. But to take a single sentence, and later a paragraph, and make it better, that yielded the small win that we all need to keep going.

Big Impact

Donald Murray defined the steps of the writing process in 1972: prewriting, drafting, revision, editing, and publishing. And while teachers rightfully spend a great deal of time prewriting, practicing the writing process more often and with less-formal writing allows students to internalize the writing process that much more. Kelly Gallagher and Penny Kittle point out the need for more practice with process. "If a student only writes 'big' essays, she is not getting enough practice to improve significantly. This pathway doesn't provide enough practice for writers" (2018, para. 5).

In about ten minutes, micro writing can provide students practice with writing as a process. It can also give writers the bones and building blocks to a great longer piece of writing.

> Back in my classroom, Andrew wrote a few sentences and a short paragraph on notecards in little jots and flourishes over a couple weeks. One afternoon, I laid them all out across his desk, taping them together. In that moment, he saw the first paper he had ever written. Those small writings made a big impact.

Kim Carlton provides professional development for educators. She previously worked as a classroom teacher, an instructional coach, a literacy coach, and a curriculum director. Kim is a Diamond-Level Abydos Writing trainer and has taught numerous summer writing institutes for teachers in grades K–12.

References

Amabile, Teresa M., and Steven J. Kramer. 2011a. "The Power of Small Wins." *Harvard Business Review*, May 2011. hbr.org/2011/05/the-power-of-small -wins.

——— 2011b. *The Progress Principle: Using Small Wins to Ignite Joy, Engagement, and Creativity at Work*. Boston: Harvard University Press.

Archer, Anita L. 2011. *Explicit Instruction: Effective and Efficient Teaching*. New York: Guilford Press.

Auray, Dea. 2020. "Writing's Role in the Science of Reading." *Empowering Writers* (blog), April 25, 2020. blog.empoweringwriters.com/blog/writings-role -in-the-science-of-reading.

Clark, Irene, and Andrea Hernandez. 2011. "Genre Awareness, Academic Argument, and Transferability." *The WAC Journal* 22: 65–78.

Cleary, Michelle N. 2014. "The Wrong Way to Teach Grammar." *The Atlantic*, February 25, 2014. theatlantic.com/education/archive/2014/02/the-wrong -way-to-teach-grammar/284014/.

Coker, David, Elizabeth Farley-Ripley, Allison Jackson, Huijing Wen, Charles MacArthur, and Austin Jennings. 2016. "Writing Instruction in First Grade: An Observational Study." *Reading and Writing: An Interdisciplinary Journal* 29: 793–832.

Davis, Lauren. 2018. "Creative Teaching and Teaching Creativity: How to Foster Creativity in the Classroom." *Psych Learning Curve: Where Psychology and Learning Connect* (blog), December 17, 2018. psychlearningcurve.org/creative -teaching-and-teaching-creativity-how-to-foster-creativity-in-the-classroom.

Ehri, Linnea C. 1995. "Phases of Development in Learning to Read Words by Sight." *Journal of Research in Reading* 18 (2): 116–125.

Ehri, Linnea C., and Sandra McCormick. 1998. "Phases of Word Learning: Implications for Instruction with Delayed and Disabled Readers." *Reading and Writing Quarterly* 14 (2): 135–163.

Ehri, Linnea C., and Margaret J. Snowling. 2004. "Developmental Variation in Word Recognition." In *Handbook of Language and Literacy: Development and Disorders*, edited by C. Addison Stone, Elaine R. Silliman, Barbara J. Ehren, and Kenn Apel, 433–460. New York: Guilford Press.

Fisher, Douglas, Nancy Frey, and John Hattie. 2016. *Visible Learning for Literacy*. Thousand Oaks, CA: Corwin.

Fleisher, Paul, Donna Fout, and Mary Ann Ready. 2003. *21st Century Writing: An Accelerated Program to Help Students Develop Their Writing Skills*. Carthage, IL: Teaching & Learning Company.

Gallagher, Kelly, and Penny Kittle. 2018. "Giving Students the Right Kind of Writing Practice." *Educational Leadership* 75 (7): 14–20.

Gartland, Lauren B., and Laura B. Smolkin. 2016. "The Histories and Mysteries of Grammar Instruction: Supporting Elementary Teachers in the Time of the Common Core." *The Reading Teacher* 69 (4): 391–399. doi.org/10.1002/trtr.1408.

Giordano, Katelynn. 2018. "My Grammar Journey." *NCTE* (blog), April 27, 2018. ncte.org/blog/2018/04/my-grammar-journey.

Gough, Philip B., and William E. Tunmer. 1986. "Decoding, Reading, and Reading Disability." *Remedial and Special Education* 7 (1): 6–10.

Graham, Steve. 2019. "Changing How Writing Is Taught." *Review of Research in Education* 43: 277–303.

Graham, Steve, Alisha Bollinger, Carol Booth Olson, Catherine D'Aoust, Charles MacArthur, Deborah McCutchen, and Natalie Olinghouse. 2012; Rev. 2018. *Teaching Elementary School Students to Be Effective Writers: A Practice Guide* (NCEE 2012-4058). Washington, DC: National Center for Education Evaluation and Regional Assistance, Institute of Education Sciences, U.S. Department of Education. ies.ed.gov/ncee/wwc/PracticeGuide/17.

Graham, Steve, Julie Bruch, Jill Fitzgerald, Linda Friedrich, Joshua Furgeson, Katie Greene, James Kim, Julia Lyskawa, Carol Booth Olson, and Claire Smither Wulsin. 2016. *Teaching Secondary Students to Write Effectively* (NCEE 2017-4002). Washington, DC: National Center for Education Evaluation and Regional Assistance (NCEE), Institute of Education Sciences, U.S. Department of Education. ies.ed.gov/ncee/wwc/PracticeGuide/22.

Graves, Donald H. 1983. *Writing: Teachers and Children at Work*. Portsmouth, NH: Heinemann.

Harrity, Erin Mary. 2012. "Incorporating Effective Grammar Instruction into the Classroom." Honors program thesis, University of Northern Iowa. scholarworks .uni.edu/hpt/40.

Hawkins, Joey, Eloise Ginty, Karen LeClaire Kurzman, Diana Leddy, and Jane Miller. 2008. *Writing for Understanding*. South Strafford, VT: Vermont Writing Collaborative.

Hochman, Judith, and Natalie Wexler. 2017. "One Sentence at a Time: The Need for Explicit Instruction in Teaching Students to Write Well." *American Educator* 21 (2): 30.

International Literacy Association. 2020. *Teaching Writing to Improve Reading Skills* [Research Advisory]. Newark, DE: International Literacy Association.

Jackson, Robin R., and Allison Zmuda. 2014. "Four (Secret) Keys to Student Engagement." *Educational Leadership* 72 (1): 18–24.

Kellogg, Ronald T., and Alison P. Whiteford. 2009. "Training Advanced Writing Skills: The Case for Deliberate Practice." *Educational Psychologist* 44 (4): 250–266.

Kilpatrick, David A. 2015. *Essentials of Assessing, Preventing, and Overcoming Reading Difficulties*. Hoboken, NJ: Wiley.

King, Jude. 2019. "The Big Power of Small Wins." *Medium*, June 7, 2019. medium .com/swlh/the-big-power-of-small-wins-c7709c9e10af.

Kittle, Penny. 2008. *Write Beside Them*. Portsmouth, NH: Heinemann.

KU Writing Center. 2021. "Prewriting Strategies." writing.ku.edu/prewriting-strategies.

Mart, Cagri Tugrul. 2013. "Teaching Grammar in Context: Why and How?" *Theory and Practice in Language Studies* 3 (1): 124–129. doi.org/10.4304 /tpls.3.1.124-129.

Moats, Louisa C. 2020. "Teaching Reading Is Rocket Science." *American Educator*, Summer 2020. www.aft.org/ae/summer2020/moats.

Murray, Donald. 1972. "Teach Writing as a Process Not Product." *The Leaflet* 54: 1–40.

National Commission on Writing. 2003. *The Neglected "R": The Need for a Writing Revolution*. New York: College Entrance Exam Board. archive.nwp .org/cs/public/download/nwp_file/21478/the-neglected-r-college-board-nwp -report.pdf?x-r=pcfile_d.

National Reading Panel (U.S.) and National Institute of Child Health and Human Development (U.S.). 2000. *Report of the National Reading Panel: Teaching Children to Read: An Evidence-based Assessment of the Scientific Research Literature on Reading and Its Implications for Reading Instruction*. Bethesda, MD: U.S. Dept. of Health and Human Services, Public Health Service, National Institutes of Health, National Institute of Child Health and Human Development.

National Writing Project and Carl Nagin. 2006. *Because Writing Matters: Improving Student Writing in Our Schools*, rev. ed. Hoboken, NJ: Wiley.

Nordquist, Richard. 2020. "Definition and Example of Syntax." *ThoughtCo.*, January 24, 2020. www.thoughtco.com/syntax-grammar-1692182.

Pimentel, Sue. 2018. "Why Doesn't Every Teacher Know the Research on Reading Instruction?" *Education Week*, October 26, 2018. www.edweek.org/teaching -learning/opinion-why-doesnt-every-teacher-know-the-research-on-reading -instruction/2018/10.

Reading Rockets. 2021. "Writing: In Practice." *Reading 101: A Guide to Teaching Reading and Writing*. www.readingrockets.org/teaching /reading101-course/welcome-reading-101.

Right Question Institute. n.d. "What Is the QFT?" Accessed February 16, 2022. rightquestion.org/what-is-the-qft.

Robinson, Lisa Kathleen, and Jay Feng. 2016. "Effect of Direct Grammar Instruction on Student Writing Skills." Paper presented at the Eastern Educational Research Association Annual Conference, Hilton Head Island, SC, February 2016.

Scarborough, Hollis S. 2001. "Connecting Early Language and Literacy to Later Reading (Dis)abilities: Evidence, Theory, and Practice." In *Handbook of Early Literacy Research*, edited by Susan B. Neuman and David K. Dickinson, 97–110. New York: Guilford Press.

Sedita, Joan. 2019. "The Strands That Are Woven into Skilled Writing." keystoliteracy.com/wp-content/uploads/2020/02/The-Strands-That-Are-Woven -Into-Skilled-WritingV2.pdf.

Seidenberg, Mark S. 2017. *Language at the Speed of Sight*. New York: Basic Books.

Smarten Up. 2021. "What Is the Writing Rope?" smarten-up.com/blog/2021/8/6 /what-is-the-writing-rope.

Tompkins, Gail E. 2013. *Literacy for the 21st Century*, 6th ed. Upper Saddle River, NJ: Pearson.

UNICEF. 2018. *Learning Through Play: Strengthening Learning Through Play in Early Childhood Education Programmes*. New York: UNICEF.

U.S. Department of Education, National Center for Education Statistics. 1998. *The Condition of Education 1998*. Washington, DC: U.S. Government Printing Office.

VanHekken, Alisa. 2021. "The Reading Rope." *Foundations in Literacy* (blog), March 4, 2021. heggerty.org/blog/the-reading-rope.

Willingham, Daniel. 2016. "Knowledge and Practice: The Real Keys to Critical Thinking." *Knowledge Matters Issue Brief* 1 (March). knowledgematterscampaign.org/wp-content/uploads/2016/05/Willingham-brief .pdf.

Glossary

active/passive voice—*active voice* means that a sentence has a subject that acts upon its verb; *passive voice* means that a subject is a recipient of a verb's action

adjective—a word that describes a noun or pronoun

adverb—a word that describes a verb, an adjective, another adverb, or a sentence and that is often used to show time, manner, place, or degree

argument—the key to an opinion, the argument is comprised of all the pieces that support the opinion and ultimately persuade others to share the opinion

article—any of a small set of words or affixes (such as *a*, *an*, and *the*) used with nouns to limit or give definiteness to the application

brainstorming—an oral and written rehearsal of ideas in which students begin to prepare for the genre in which they will write

characters—people, animals, beings, creatures, or things in a story; the characters perform the actions and speak the dialogue that make the story progress

claims/counterclaims—claims are arguments; counterclaims are opposing arguments

clause—a word grouping that contains a subject and a verb; *independent clauses* convey complete meanings and can stand alone as simple sentences; *dependent clauses* do not express complete ideas on their own and must be paired with another clause

clustering—a way to record thoughts and observations for a piece of writing after students have chosen a topic

cohesion—cohesion is when the prose is clear and easy to understand, with all ideas presented in an orderly manner and tied together in a logical way; the use of explicit techniques to indicate the relationships among different parts of the text

complex sentence—a sentence with at least one independent clause and one dependent clause

compound sentence—a sentence with at least two independent clauses and no dependent clauses; the independent clauses can be linked by a comma, semicolon, dash, or conjunction

compound-complex sentence—a sentence with at least two independent clauses, and at least one dependent clause

conjunction—a word that joins two grammatical elements of the same sentence or construction; words that illustrate the meaning between two clauses, such as *and*, *but*, or *or*

diagramming—a visual organizational prewriting activity to help see relationships; writers create a concept map of how different elements fit together

direct object—the thing that is being acted upon by the subject; it receives the action of the verb

drafting—the stage of the writing process when a preliminary version of text is created

editing—the stage of the writing process when changes are made to ensure the writing adheres to the conventions of written English, including grammar, spelling, word choice, punctuation, and formatting

evidence (support)—facts, documentation, or testimony used to strengthen a claim, support an argument, or reach a conclusion

expanding [sentences]—the process of adding more words, phrases, or clauses

facts and details—facts are things that are known to be true; they often answer the questions *who, what, where, when, why,* or *how.* Details are examples that expand on an idea, including descriptions, quotes, analyses, statistics, anecdotes, or reasons.

freewriting—a prewriting strategy that involves filling a sheet of paper with ideas, without worrying about grammar, spelling, or even coherence

grammar, usage, and mechanics—*grammar* is the structure of written or spoken language, the parts of speech, and how they combine to form sentences; *usage* is the way words and phrases are used to produce coherent sentences; *mechanics* refers to conventions of written language, such as capitalization, punctuation, and spelling

informational/explanatory—factual writing that demonstrates comprehension of a topic, concept, process, or procedure

mentor text—a piece of writing that serves as a model or an illustrative example that teachers and students read and reread for different purposes; any format of writing can serve as a mentor text: poem, argumentative essay, introduction, transition sentences

narrative—a story, usually of a personal experience; a spoken or written account of connected events

narrator—a character who recounts the events of a story or novel

noun—a word that is the name of something (such as a person, animal, place, thing, quality, idea, or action) and is typically used in a sentence as the subject or object of a verb or as the object of a preposition

opinion—a personal belief or judgment; what an individual thinks about something

organizing—the arrangement of ideas, incidents, evidence, or details in a perceptible order in a paragraph, essay, or speech

outlining—a plan for the paper that will help writers organize and structure their ideas in a way that effectively communicates the ideas to readers and supports the thesis statement

participle—a type of word derived from a verb that is used for a variety of purposes, such as an adjective or to construct verb tenses. For a regular verb, a *past participle* is typically formed by adding –*ed* to the end of the root form of a verb. *Present participles* are formed by adding –*ing* to the root forms of verbs.

phrase—a group of two or more words functioning as a meaningful unit within a sentence or clause; a phrase does not contain a subject-verb pairing

predicate—the part of the sentence that usually contains a verb and describes the subject or shows action

preposition—a word or group of words that is used with a noun, pronoun, or noun phrase to show direction, location, or time or to introduce an object

prewriting—the stage of the writing process when writers develop goals, generate ideas, gather information, organize ideas, and develop a logical structure

pronoun—a word (such as *I, he, she, you, it, we,* or *they*) that is used instead of a noun or noun phrase

publication—a final product that is shared in written and/or oral form

recursive—a process that is looped so that it is repeated and revisited

revision—the stage of the writing process when the author reviews, alters, and amends the content of writing by adding, deleting, or rearranging to clarify or enhance meaning

sequence of events—events that come one after the other in a particular order. In a story, these may be the beginning, middle, and end; in informational writing, these may be steps in a process; in persuasive writing, the sequence may include causes and effects.

simple sentence—a sentence containing a subject and a verb and expressing a complete thought; it might contain other components as well, but only requires a subject and verb to be a simple sentence

subject—the person, place, or thing that is performing the action of the sentence; the subject represents what or whom the sentence is about

subject/predicate—two parts of a sentence; the *subject* is what or whom the sentence is about, and the *predicate* is a clause that tells something about the subject, what it is doing, or a description about it

syntactic awareness—the ability to monitor the relationships among the words in a sentence to understand while reading or composing orally or in writing

syntax—the order in which words are arranged in a spoken or written sentence; the arrangement of words and phrases to create well-formed sentences

temporal words—time-related transitions

tense—the tense of a verb tells you when something existed or happened. There are three main tenses: *present, past,* and *future. Present* describes things that are currently happening; *past* describes things that have already happened; *future* refers to events that have not happened but that are due to happen.

transitions—bridges between parts of a sentence, between sentences, or between paragraphs; transitions enable the reader to make logical connections between ideas and carry a thought through for cohesiveness

verb—words that show an action (*sing*), occurrence (*develop*), or state of being (*exist*)

Index

f denotes figure

W